UNDERSTANDING AND USING

English Grammar

FOURTH EDITION

WORKBOOK

Volume A

Betty S. Azar
Rachel Spack Koch
Stacy A. Hagen

PEARSON
Longman

Understanding and Using English Grammar, Fourth Edition Workbook, Volume A

Pearson Education, 10 Bank Street, White Plains, NY 10606

Staff credits: The people who made up the *Understanding and Using English Grammar, Fourth Edition, Workbook Volume A* team, representing editorial, production, design, and manufacturing, are Dave Dickey, Christine Edmonds, Ann France, Margo Grant, Amy McCormick, and Robert Ruvo.

Text composition: S4Carlisle Publishing Services
Text font: 10.5/12 Plantin

Illustrations: Don Martinetti—pages 20, 21, 42, 50; Chris Pavely—pages 4, 15, 19, 47, 60, 67, 69, 72, 80, 98, 111

ISBN 10: 0-13-241544-5
ISBN 13: 978-0-13-241544-6

Printed in the United States of America
1 2 3 4 5 6 7 8 9 10—DBH—14 13 12 11 10 09

Contents

Preface

The *Understanding and Using English Grammar Workbook* is a place for students to explore and practice English grammar on their own. It is a place where they can test and fine-tune their understandings of English structures and improve their abilities to use English meaningfully and correctly. All of the exercises have been designed for independent study, but this book is also a resource for teachers who need exercise material for additional classwork, homework, testing, or individualized instruction.

The *Workbook* is keyed to the explanatory grammar charts found in *Understanding and Using English Grammar, Fourth Edition,* a classroom teaching text for students of English as a second or foreign language, as well as in the accompanying *Chartbook,* a reference grammar with no exercises.

The answers to the practices can be found in the *Answer Key* in the back of the *Workbook.* Its pages are perforated so that they can be detached to make a separate booklet. However, if teachers want to use the *Workbook* as a classroom teaching text, the *Answer Key* can be removed at the beginning of the term.

A special *Workbook* section called *Phrasal Verbs,* not available in the main text, is included in the *Appendix.* This section provides a reference list of common phrasal verbs along with a variety of exercises for independent practice.

Chapter 1
Overview of Verb Tenses

▶ **Practice 1. Preview.** (Charts 1-1 → 1-5)
Write the correct form of the verbs in parentheses to complete the sentences.

1. A: I'm going to ask you some questions so that we can practice verb tenses. What do you do every day before you come to class? Name one thing.

   B: I (*eat*) _____*eat*_____ breakfast.

2. A: What did you do last night? Name three separate activities.

   B: Last night I (*eat*) _____ dinner. Then I (*visit*) _____ some friends, and later I (*write*) _____ a couple of letters.

3. A: What are you doing right now? What activity is in progress right now, at this exact moment?

   B: Right now I (*talk*) _____ to you. I (*answer*) _____ your questions.

4. A: Where were you at this exact time yesterday? And what activity was in progress then?

   B: Let me think. At this time yesterday, I was at the bookstore. I (*look*) _____ _____ for the books I needed to buy for this class.

5. A: How many questions have I asked since we began this exercise?

   B: I think you (*ask*) _____ me five or six questions since we began this exercise.

6. A: What have you been doing for the past five minutes? In other words, what activity began five minutes ago and has been in progress from then until now?

   B: I (*talk*) _____ to you for the past five minutes. I started talking to you five minutes ago, and I am still talking to you.

7. A: Where will you be tomorrow morning?

   B: I (*be*) _____ in class tomorrow morning.

8. A: What will you be doing at this exact time tomorrow? In other words, what activity will be in progress at this exact same time tomorrow?

   B: Right now I am sitting in the classroom. And at this exact time tomorrow, I (*sit*) _____ in the classroom.

9. A: What had you done by the time you got to class today? In other words, what is one activity that you had completed before you arrived in class today?

   B: Well, for one thing, I (*eat*) _____ breakfast by the time I got to class today.

10. A: What will you have done by the time you go to bed tonight? Name one activity that you will have completed before you go to bed tonight.

    B: I (*eat*) _____ dinner by the time I go to bed tonight.

▶ **Practice 2. Verb tenses: overview.** (Charts 1-1 → 1-5)
This is a calendar of the month of February. For each item, write the date or dates that the text refers to.

February						
Sun	**Mon**	**Tue**	**Wed**	**Thu**	**Fri**	**Sat**
1	2	3	4	5	6	7
8	9	10	11	12	13	14
15	16	17	18	19	20	21
22	23	24	25	26	27	28

1. Today is Wednesday, February 11th. We play tennis on Saturdays. These are the dates we play tennis in February: February __7th__, __14th__, __21st__, and __28th__.

2. Today is Wednesday, February 4th. We're going to play tennis on Saturday. We're going to play tennis on February _____.

3. Today is Wednesday, February 4th. It rained yesterday. It rained on February _____.

4. Today is Wednesday, February 4th. It's been raining since Monday. It has rained on these days: February _____, _____, and _____.

5. Today is Friday, February 13th. It's beautiful today, but it had been raining for three days. It rained on February _____, _____, and _____.

6. Today is Friday, February 13th. It's not going to rain during the weekend. It won't rain on February _____ and _____.

7. Today is Saturday, February 21st. We've been here for exactly two weeks. We arrived here on February _____.

8. Today is Monday, February 23rd. Our singing group meets every Tuesday evening, and we sing from 7:00 to 9:00 P.M. I will be singing with my group on the evening of February _____.

▶ **Practice 3. The simple tenses and the progressive tenses.** (Charts 1-1 and 1-2)
Circle the correct verb to complete each sentence.

1. It (*is raining / rains*) every day in August.

2. Uncle Joe (*visited / visits*) us last month.

3. Our team (*will win* / *wins*) the soccer game tomorrow.

4. Nick (*watches* / *is watching*) an action movie on TV now.

5. Tomorrow at this time we (*will be flying* / *are flying*) over the Atlantic Ocean.

6. Tina! I (*was thinking* / *am thinking*) of you just a minute ago when the phone rang!

7. I know you, Aunt Martha. You're never going to retire. You (*are working* / *will be working*) at your computer even when you are 90 years old.

8. At 9:00 P.M. last night, all the children (*go* / *went*) to bed. At 10:00 P.M. they (*slept* / *were sleeping*).

9. Uh-oh. Look! Mr. Anton (*fell* / *was falling*) down on the ice. Mr. Anton! Don't move! We (*help* / *will help*) you!

10. A: Why is the beach closed today?

    B: There are sharks in the water! They (*swim* / *are swimming*) near the shore!

▶ **Practice 4. The perfect tenses.** (Chart 1-3)
Circle the correct verb to complete each sentence.

1. I (*have* / *had*) already seen the movie twice.

2. I (*have* / *had*) already seen the movie, so I didn't want to see it again.

3. Guy (*has been* / *was*) a professor at this university since 2001. He's going to be chairman of the English department next year.

4. Fred (*has been* / *was*) a judge in the Supreme Court of this state for 21 years until he retired last year.

5. On the 14th of next month, my grandparents are going to celebrate their 50th wedding anniversary. They (*will have been* / *had been*) married for 50 years.

6. Rafael and Sue live in Springfield. They (*lived* / *have lived*) there all their lives.

7. Ann and Sid moved to Chicago. Before that, they (*have* / *had*) lived in this town all their lives.

8. Sorry, Mr. Wu. You (*have* / *will have*) missed your flight! The plane left just two minutes ago.

9. Jan speaks excellent English. He (*had* / *has*) studied English in school for twelve years before he came here.

10. We were too late to have dinner at the restaurant. When we got there, it (*has* / *had*) already closed for the night.

▶ **Practice 5. The perfect progressive tenses.** (Chart 1-4)
Circle the correct verb to complete each sentence.

1. I'm thirsty, aren't you? We (*have* / *had*) been driving for four hours. Let's stop for a cold drink soon.

2. When is the rain going to stop? It (*has been* / *was*) raining for two days.

3. When Greta graduates from medical school next year, she (*will be* / *will have been*) studying for twenty years!

4. After Jim and Kim (*have* / *had*) been going out together for seven years, they finally got married last month.

5. You (*has / have*) been working in this office for only two months, and you've already gotten a raise? That's great!

6. Stan finally quit playing professional tennis after he broke his ankle two months ago. He (*has / had*) been playing for twenty years.

7. Well, it's good to be on this plane. Finally! We (*have been waiting / will have been waiting*) almost two hours!

8. Wake Maria up now. She (*had / has*) been sleeping for three hours. That's a very long nap.

9. The police officer gave Pedro a ticket because he (*has / had*) been speeding.

▶ **Practice 6. The perfect and the perfect progressive tenses.** (Charts 1-3 and 1-4)
Choose the sentence that means the same as the given sentence(s). Write the letter of the sentence.

1. We've been watching TV all night. _____
   a. We are still watching TV.
   b. We watched TV until a little while ago.

2. I've already done my homework. _____
   a. I'm still doing my homework.
   b. I've finished my homework.

3. The baby was crying when I picked him up. _____
   a. First the baby cried. Then I picked him up.
   b. First I picked up the baby. Then he cried.

4. The baby cried when I picked him up. _____
   a. First the baby cried. Then I picked him up.
   b. First I picked up the baby. Then he cried.

5. Don't wake me up when you get home at midnight. I'll be sleeping then. _____
   a. I'm going to go to sleep before midnight.
   b. I'm going to go to sleep after midnight.

6. I'm not going home for the summer break. I'll be studying. _____
   a. I have a lot of studying to do.
   b. I don't have a lot of studying to do.

7. At the beginning of the new year, I'll start a new job. _____
   a. I'll start a new job before the new year begins.
   b. I'll start a new job when the new year begins.

8. By the beginning of the new year, I will have started my new job. _____
   a. I'll start a new job before the new year begins.
   b. I'll start a new job when the new year begins.

9. Joe and his family had cleaned the whole house before his parents arrived. _____
   a. The house was already clean when his parents arrived.
   b. The house was not yet clean when his parents arrived.

► **Practice 7. Verb tenses.** (Charts 1-1 → 1-5)
Write the correct form of the verbs in parentheses to complete the sentences.

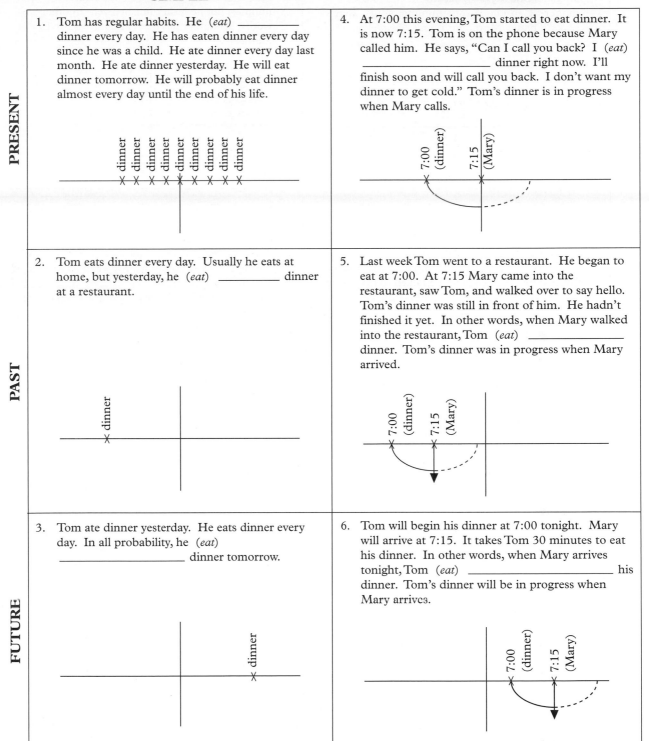

SIMPLE   **PROGRESSIVE**

PRESENT

1. Tom has regular habits. He (*eat*) _____ dinner every day. He has eaten dinner every day since he was a child. He ate dinner every day last month. He ate dinner yesterday. He will eat dinner tomorrow. He will probably eat dinner almost every day until the end of his life.

4. At 7:00 this evening, Tom started to eat dinner. It is now 7:15. Tom is on the phone because Mary called him. He says, "Can I call you back? I (*eat*) _____ dinner right now. I'll finish soon and will call you back. I don't want my dinner to get cold." Tom's dinner is in progress when Mary calls.

PAST

2. Tom eats dinner every day. Usually he eats at home, but yesterday, he (*eat*) _____ dinner at a restaurant.

5. Last week Tom went to a restaurant. He began to eat at 7:00. At 7:15 Mary came into the restaurant, saw Tom, and walked over to say hello. Tom's dinner was still in front of him. He hadn't finished it yet. In other words, when Mary walked into the restaurant, Tom (*eat*) _____ dinner. Tom's dinner was in progress when Mary arrived.

FUTURE

3. Tom ate dinner yesterday. He eats dinner every day. In all probability, he (*eat*) _____ dinner tomorrow.

6. Tom will begin his dinner at 7:00 tonight. Mary will arrive at 7:15. It takes Tom 30 minutes to eat his dinner. In other words, when Mary arrives tonight, Tom (*eat*) _____ his dinner. Tom's dinner will be in progress when Mary arrives.

(continued on next page)

PERFECT	PERFECT PROGRESSIVE

PRESENT

7. Tom finished eating dinner at 7:30 tonight. It is now 8:00, and his mother has just come into the kitchen. She says, "What would you like for dinner? Can I cook something for you?" Tom says, "Thanks Mom, but I (*eat, already*) _____ dinner."

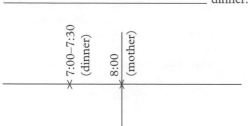

10. Tom began to eat dinner at 7:00 tonight. It is now, at this moment, 7:15. Tom (*eat*) _____ _____ his dinner for 15 minutes, but he hasn't finished yet. In other words, his dinner has been in progress for 15 minutes.

PAST

8. Yesterday Tom cooked his own dinner. He began at 7:00 and finished at 7:30. At 8:00 his mother came into the kitchen. She offered to cook some food for Tom, but he (*eat, already*) _____ _____. In other words, Tom had finished his dinner before he talked to his mother.

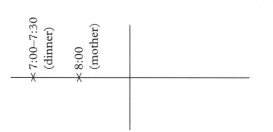

11. Last week Tom went to a restaurant. He began to eat at 7:00. At 7:15 Mary came into the restaurant, saw Tom, and walked over to say hello. Tom's dinner was still in front of him. He hadn't finished it yet. In other words, when Mary walked into the restaurant, Tom (*eat*) _____ dinner. Tom's dinner was in progress when Mary arrived.

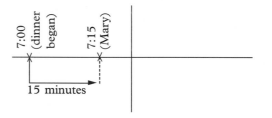

FUTURE

9. Tomorrow Tom will begin dinner at 7:00 and finish at 7:30. His mother will come into the kitchen at 8:00. In other words, Tom (*eat, already*) _____

dinner by the time his mother walks into the kitchen.

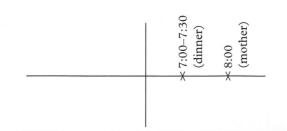

12. Tonight Tom will go to a restaurant. He will begin to eat at 7:00. At 7:15 Mary will come into the restaurant, see Tom, and walk over to say hello. Tom's dinner will still be in front of him. He won't have finished it yet. In other words, when Mary walks into the restaurant, Tom (*eat*) _____ _____ dinner for 15 minutes. Tom's dinner will have been in progress for 15 minutes by the time Mary arrives.

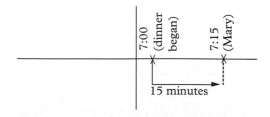

▶ **Practice 8. Verb tenses.** (Charts 1-1 → 1-5)
Circle the phrase that correctly describes each sentence.

1. He is eating dinner.   daily habit   (at this time)   in the past
2. We ate a huge dinner.   in the future   at this time   in the past
3. She doesn't eat lunch.   daily habit   at this time   in the past
4. I've been busy.   past and present   past only   only today
5. Sam spoke to Anna.   past and present   past only   daily habit
6. They were studying.   past and present   at this time   in the past
7. They're sleeping.   daily habit   at this time   in the past
8. I'll see you there.   in the future   daily habit   at this time
9. Sue plays the violin.   in the future   daily habit   at this time
10. Tina played the drums.   daily habit   at this time   in the past

▶ **Practice 9. Verb tenses.** (Charts 1-1 → 1-5)
Circle the letter of each word or phrase that can complete the sentence. More than one completion may be correct.

1. We will be there _____.
    a. now   b. soon   c. next week

2. It's raining really hard _____.
    a. right now   b. last week   c. tomorrow

3. Shhh! The movie is beginning _____.
    a. daily   b. now   c. right now

4. The newspaper hasn't come _____.
    a. tomorrow   b. all day   c. since Monday

5. We are enjoying the nice weather _____.
    a. now   b. this week   c. sometimes

6. I am going to study _____.
    a. last night   b. next month   c. this weekend

7. John has been sleeping _____.
    a. since 9:00   b. all day   c. for two hours

8. He worked hard _____.
    a. last week   b. now   c. yesterday

9. Carlos was studying _____.
    a. at midnight   b. when we came   c. in a week

10. We'll see you _____.
    a. tomorrow   b. a minute ago   c. in the morning

11. I'll be talking to you _____.
    a. soon   b. now   c. in a few days

► **Practice 10. Verb tenses.** (Charts 1-1 → 1-5)
Write the letters of all the phrases that can complete each sentence.

1. Every day I _____ .
   a. memorize new vocabulary
   b. am memorizing new vocabulary
   c. was memorizing new vocabulary

2. Right now it _____ .
   a. is snowing
   b. was snowing
   c. snows

3. By the time the plane lands, _____ .
   a. I have finished my book
   b. I will have finished my book
   c. I had been finishing my book

4. Tomorrow at this time _____ .
   a. we will have arrived home
   b. we will be arriving home
   c. we arrived home

5. Pretty soon the weather _____ .
   a. will turn cold
   b. is going to turn cold
   c. will be turning cold

6. While you were sleeping, _____ .
   a. your mom stopped by
   b. your mom has stopped by
   c. your mom was stopping by

7. Before you got here, _____ .
   a. I had been cleaning my room
   b. I am cleaning my room
   c. I will have cleaned my room

8. They had left the restaurant _____ .
   a. before we arrived
   b. after we arrived
   c. by the time we arrived

► **Practice 11. Spelling of *-ing* forms.** (Chart 1-6)
Write the *-ing* form of each verb in the correct column.

	Just add *-ing* to the simple form.	**Drop the final *-e* and add *-ing*.**	**Double the final letter and add *-ing*.**
1. arrive		*arriving*	
2. copy	*copying*		
3. cut			*cutting*
4. enjoy			
5. fill			
6. happen			
7. hope			
8. leave			
9. make			
10. rub			
11. stay			
12. stop			
13. take			
14. win			
15. work			

Write the **-*ed*** form for each verb in the correct column.

	Just add -*ed* to the simple form.	Add -*d* only.	Double the final letter and add -*ed*.	Change the -*y* to -*i* and add -*ed*.
1. bother	bothered			
2. copy				copied
3. enjoy				
4. fasten				
5. fear				
6. occur				
7. pat				
8. play				
9. rain				
10. refer				
11. reply				
12. return				
13. scare				
14. try				
15. walk				

Write the **-ing** and **-ed** form for each word in the correct column.

	-ing	-ed
1. prefer	*preferring*	*preferred*
2. study		
3. work		
4. offer		
5. kiss		
6. play		
7. faint		
8. allow		
9. stop		
10. tie		
11. die		
12. fold		
13. try		
14. decide		
15. hop		

► **Practice 14. Chapter review.** (Chapter 1)

Read the conversation between a new teacher and his students on the first day of class. Write the correct form of the verbs in parentheses to complete the conversation.

Part I. The first day of the new semester.

TEACHER: Good morning, students. I'm your new music teacher, Tom Piazza.

STUDENT 1: Hello, Mr. Piazza. How (*you, spell*) _____ your name?
                                                                    1

MR. PIAZZA: I (*spell*) _____ it almost like *pizza,* but it (*have*) _____
                              2   3

an extra "A" in the middle.

STUDENT 2: Where (*you, be*) _____ from, Mr. Piazza?
                                          4

MR. PIAZZA: Well, I (*be*) _____ Italian. You can tell that by the name. I was
                            5

born in Italy, but I (*live*) _____ there for only two years as a
                                    6

child. My parents (*move*) _____ to New York with the whole
                                    7

family when I was just two years old.

STUDENT 3: Oh, (*you, grow*) _____ up in New York then?
8

MR. PIAZZA: Yes, I did. I grew up in New York City.

STUDENT 4: So when (*you, come*) _____ here to Springfield?
9

MR. PIAZZA: Just two weeks ago. I (*arrive*) _____ here just two weeks ago!
10

I (*be*) _____ here for two weeks.
11

STUDENT 5: Only two weeks! Well, (*you, like*) _____ Springfield?
12

MR. PIAZZA: I do. It seems very nice. Right now I (*stay*) _____
13

downtown in the PriceWise Hotel. I (*look*) _____ for an
14

apartment near this school now. In fact, I (*look*) _____
15

_____ for an apartment for two weeks. I hope that I

(*find*) _____ one soon.
16

Part II. Two weeks later.

STUDENT: (*you, find*) _____ an apartment yet, Mr. Piazza?
17

MR. PIAZZA: Yes, I have. As you know, I (*look*) _____ for one for the
18

past two weeks, and then over the weekend, I found a nice one.

STUDENT: Great! When (*you, move*) _____ in?
19

MR. PIAZZA: Next weekend. Usually I (*give*) _____ piano lessons all day on
20

Saturdays, but next Saturday I won't be giving lessons. Next Saturday and

Sunday — all day — I (*move*) _____ all my things
21

into my new place. It will take the whole weekend, I'm sure. But next Monday at

this time, I (*move*) _____ everything into my new
22

apartment. I (*be*) _____ very happy here in Springfield in the
23

future, I know.

Chapter 2
Present and Past; Simple and Progressive

▶ **Practice 1. The simple present and the present progressive.** (Charts 2-1 and 2-2)
Complete the sentences. Write the simple present or the present progressive form of the verbs in parentheses.

1. The sun (*set*) _____ *sets* _____ in the west every evening.

2. Look! The sun (*set*) _____ behind the mountain now. How beautiful!

3. The football players (*practice*) _____ on the field right now.

4. The football players (*practice*) _____ on the field every afternoon.

5. I always (*listen*) _____ to the radio when I'm in my car.

6. The traffic is bad today, but it isn't bothering me. I (*listen*) _____ to

    my favorite morning talk show with Jack LaLoule, who is very funny.

7. Sam and Lara (*talk*) _____ on the phone every night.

8. Sam and Lara (*talk*) _____ on the phone right now, so I can't call

    Lara. Her line is busy.

9. I'll call you back in a little while. We (*eat*) _____ dinner right now.

10. My grandparents usually (*eat*) _____ dinner early. They often go out to

    their favorite restaurant for the early dinner special at 5:30.

▶ **Practice 2. The simple present and the present progressive.** (Charts 2-1 and 2-2)
Circle the correct verb.

1. Because of the force of gravity, objects (*fall / are falling*) down and not up.

2. It's autumn! The leaves (*fall / are falling*), and winter will soon be here.

3. Coffee (*grows / is growing*) in mountainous areas, not in deserts.

4. Oh, you (*grow / are growing*) so fast, Johnny! Soon you'll be taller than your dad.

5. Near the Arctic Circle, the sun (*shines / is shining*) for more than twenty hours a day at the
   beginning of the summer.

6. It's a beautiful day! The sun (*shines / is shining*) and the birds (*sing / are singing*).

7. Maria is a professional singer. She (*sings / is singing*) in the opera every season.

8. Olga likes mysteries. She (*reads / is reading*) one mystery book every week.

9. Hello, Sarah? I (*call / am calling*) you from my car. I'm going to be a little late for lunch.

► **Practice 3. The simple present and the present progressive.** (Charts 2-1 and 2-2)
Complete the sentences. Write either the simple present or the present progressive form of the verbs in the list. Use each verb only once.

belong	bleed	mean	shrink	try
bite	fail	✓ own	sleep	

1. The bank lent us money for a down payment, so now we _____own_____ the house we used to rent.

2. Shhh! I _____ to concentrate. I can't hear myself think with all that noise going on.

3. This book is mine. That one _____ to Pierre.

4. Shhh! The baby _____. We don't want to wake him up.

5. *Singular* _____ "one."

6. That sweater won't fit you if you wash it in hot water. Wool _____ in hot water.

7. Look at Joan. She _____ her fingernails. She must be nervous.

8. A: Juan! What's the matter with your hand? It _____.
   B: I just cut it when I was using a knife. It's not serious. I'll wash it and put a bandage on it.

9. A: My grades in school are terrible this term. I _____ three of my courses.
   B: Maybe you can improve them before the end of the term if you start studying.

► **Practice 4. Non-progressive verbs.** (Chart 2-3)
Write the letter of the correct completion.

1. There you are! Behind the tree! I _____ you.
   a. see
   b. am seeing

2. My mother's hearing has been getting worse for several months. She _____ a specialist right now.
   a. sees
   b. is seeing

3. Do you see that man? I _____ him. He was my high school English teacher.
   a. recognize
   b. am recognizing

4. My favorite actor _____ at the Paramount Theater.
   a. currently appears
   b. is currently appearing

5. A: Is my voice loud enough?
   B: Yes, _____.
   a. I hear you
   b. I am hearing you

6. A: Aren't you having any coffee?

   B: No, _____.
      a. I prefer tea
      b. I'm preferring tea

7. A: What's on your mind?

   B: I _____.
      a. think about my family
      b. am thinking about my family

8. A: Did you make a decision yet?

   B: No, _____.
      a. I need your opinion
      b. I'm needing your opinion

9. A: Why are you staring at me?

   B: _____.
      a. You resemble your mom so much
      b. You are resembling your mom so much

10. A: There's Dr. Jones on a motorcycle! Do you believe it? _____.

    B: a. Yeah, he owns several
       b. Yeah, he is owning several

▶ **Practice 5. The present progressive to describe a temporary state.** (Chart 2-3, 2nd footnote)

Circle the letter of the correct completion. If the situation describes a temporary state, choose the present progressive.

1. My husband and I are short, but our children _____.
   (a.) are tall   b. are being tall

2. Jane's an intelligent woman, but she won't see a doctor about those headaches she has. She _____ now.
   a. is foolish   (b.) is being foolish

3. The teacher spoke harshly to the children because they were too noisy, so now they _____.
   a. are quiet   b. are being quiet

4. Don't eat that chocolate dessert. It _____.
   a. is not healthy   b. is not being healthy

5. Timmy! Those are bad words you're saying to Mr. Hawkes. You _____.
   a. are not polite   b. are not being polite

6. I'm worried about Jeff. He has pneumonia. He _____.
   a. is very ill   b. is being very ill

► **Practice 6. Regular and irregular verbs.** (Charts 2-4 and 2-5)
Read the passage about *Sputnik*.

History changed on October 4th, 1957 when the Soviet Union successfully launched* *Sputnik I*. The world's first artificial satellite was about the size of a beach ball (58 cm., or 22.8 in.), weighed only 83.6 kg., or 183.9 pounds, and took about 98 minutes to orbit the Earth on its elliptical path. That launch ushered in** new political, military, technological, and scientific developments. While the *Sputnik* launch was a single event, it marked the start of the space age and the U.S.–Soviet Union space race.

Part I. Circle the eight past tense verbs in the passage.

Part II. Answer the questions according to the information in the passage. Circle "T" if the statement is true. Circle "F" if the statement is false.

1. The Soviet Union launched the first artificial satellite.   T   F
2. The first satellite was about the size of a golf ball.   T   F
3. The first orbit around the Earth took about an hour and a half.   T   F
4. *Sputnik* went into space several times.   T   F
5. This first launch was the beginning of the space age and the space race.   T   F

► **Practice 7. Regular and irregular verbs.** (Charts 2-4 and 2-5)
Complete the sentences. Write the simple past tense of the verbs in **bold**.

Part I. Regular verbs: The simple past and past participle end in *-ed*.

1. Sandy **works** at a bakery. She _____worked_____ there last Saturday.

2. Burt often **listens** to old Beatles songs. He _____listened_____ to some last night too.

3. Ana and Juan **study** English in a group on Saturday mornings. Last Saturday, they _____ the irregular past tense verbs.

4. It **rains** every afternoon in the summer. Yesterday it _____ all afternoon and all night too.

Part II. Irregular verbs: The simple past and past participle do not end in *-ed*.

5. Watch out! Those glasses **break** easily. Uh-oh . . . one glass just _____ .

6. Nowadays, I occasionally **swim** for exercise when I have time, but I _____ every day when I was a child.

7. Lightning sometimes **hits** trees in this area. In the last storm, a lightning bolt _____ my neighbor's tree and caused it to fall on his house.

---

*launch = to start something, usually something big or important.
**usher in = to introduce.

▶ **Practice 8. Irregular verbs.** (Chart 2-5)
Complete the sentences. Write the simple past tense of the verbs in **bold**.

Group 1.

1. This year corn **costs** a lot more than it _____ last year.

2. Gail generally **shuts** the door very quietly, but tonight she _____ it with a loud bang because she was very angry.

3. I usually **cut** my daughter's hair myself, but last week I was sick and she went to a hairdresser. He _____ it too short, and she wasn't happy.

4. Andrew moves from job to job. Normally, he works for about a year and then **quits**, but on this last job, he _____ after only one month.

Group 2.

5. Sometimes I **forget** things. Yesterday I _____ to take my keys with me, and when I got home, I couldn't get into my house.

6. Presidents **choose** their assistants and their cabinet officers. Last week the president _____ the chief financial officer of a major bank to be the secretary of the treasury.

7. I am a history major. I **take** a lot of history courses. Last semester I _____ Medieval European History and Modern African History.

8. Jenny always **gives** generous presents. Last year she _____ me a beautiful silver picture frame from Mexico.

▶ **Practice 9. Irregular verbs.** (Chart 2-5)
Complete the sentences. Write the simple past tense of the verbs in **bold**.

Group 3.

1. The concert usually **begins** on time, but tonight it _____ ten minutes late.

2. The opera star generally **sings** beautifully, but last night he _____ poorly because he was getting a cold.

3. Joe **runs** in marathons. Last year he _____ in the New York Marathon.

4. Keisha usually **drinks** green tea. At our house, we didn't have any green tea, so she _____ decaffeinated coffee.

Group 4.

5. I always **buy** fresh vegetables on the weekend. Last Saturday I _____ fresh asparagus.

6. Mr. Joseph **teaches** Spanish in high school. He _____ my mother Spanish in the same high school 25 years ago.

7. Our basketball team doesn't **win** many games, but we _____ last Friday night.

8. The other team is an excellent team, and they rarely **lose** a game. But they _____ the game last Friday night.

9. A: Isn't Helen still here? She usually **leaves** after six, doesn't she?

   B: Not today. She _____ early for a dentist's appointment.

10. A: Don't tell this to Grandma. Bad news about the family always **upsets** her.

    B: I told her already. And it's true — the bad news _____ her. She cried.

▶ **Practice 10. Irregular verbs.** (Chart 2-5)
Complete the sentences. Write the simple past tense of the verbs in **bold**.

Group 5.

1. I **know** the whole Grant family. I know their aunts, uncles, and cousins, and I _____ their grandparents long ago.

2. Tom is a pilot. He **flies** across the Atlantic Ocean regularly. Last month he _____ to Australia for the first time.

3. I rarely **do** all of my homework. Last night I _____ about half of it before I went to bed for the night.

4. My friends and I usually **see** a movie on Friday nights. Last Friday night we _____ the new science-fiction movie, *Robot Planet*.

Group 6.

5. Joanna is an excellent runner. She **runs** in the Olympic Games. She _____ in the Olympic Games in Athens in 2004 and in Beijing in 2008.

6. Aunt Jessie rarely **comes** to our house. But last year she _____ for my brother's wedding.

7. When you mix red paint and yellow paint, it **becomes** orange paint. Yesterday I mixed yellow paint with blue paint, and it _____ green.

Group 7.

8. A: Your mother **is** an English teacher, right?

   B: Well, she _____ an English teacher until she retired. Now she writes books to teach people English.

9. A: You **go** to the math review sessions on Monday nights, don't you?

   B: Yes, I do. I _____ to the review session last night.

Group 8.

10. Some children **dream** of becoming astronauts. I didn't. I always _____ of becoming a famous writer.

11. Musicians **learn** to play instruments when they are very young. My cousin _____ to play the violin when she was only four years old.

12. Fires **burn** quickly in this dry weather. Last month a fire _____ out of control for a week in the national park.

13. Be careful! The milk is going to **spill**! Uh-oh. Too late. It _____ all over the rug.

▶ **Practice 11. Irregular verbs.** (Chart 2-5)
Write the simple past and the past participle forms of the verbs.

Simple Form	Simple Past	Past Participle
1. sell	*sold*	*sold*
2. buy		
3. begin		
4. have		
5. catch		
6. quit		
7. find		
8. make		
9. take		
10. break		
11. come		
12. lose		
13. sleep		
14. build		
15. fight		

► **Practice 12. Irregular verbs.** (Chart 2-5)
Complete the verb chart. Write the missing simple present, simple past, or past participle forms.

Simple Form	Simple Past	Past Participle
1. understand	*understood*	*understood*
2.	spent	
3. let		
4.		seen
5. teach		
6.	spoke	
7.		gone
8. pay		
9.		forgotten
10.	wrote	
11. fall		
12.	felt	
13.		left
14.	upset	
15.		flown

► **Practice 13. Irregular verbs.** (Chart 2-5)
In this exercise, a police reporter interviews the victim of a theft. The victim answers the questions, using a past tense verb. Write the victim's words.

1. REPORTER: So, a thief broke into your home last night?

   VICTIM: Yes, a thief _____ into my home last night.

2. REPORTER: Did he steal anything?

   VICTIM: Yes, he _____ some things.

3. REPORTER: Did you know he was in your apartment?

   VICTIM: Yes, I _____ he was in my apartment.

4. REPORTER: Did you hear him come in?

   VICTIM: Yes, I _____ him come in.

5. REPORTER: Did the police come?

   VICTIM: Yes, the police _____ .

6. REPORTER: Did your hands shake when you called the police?

   VICTIM: Yes, my hands _____ when I called them.

7. REPORTER: Did he hide in your garden?

    VICTIM: Yes, he _____ in my garden.

8. REPORTER: Did the police find him?

    VICTIM: Yes, the police _____ him.

9. REPORTER: Did they fight with him?

    VICTIM: Yes, they _____ with him.

10. REPORTER: Did he run away?

    VICTIM: Yes, he _____ away.

11. REPORTER: Did they shoot at him?

    VICTIM: Yes, they _____ at him.

12. REPORTER: Did they catch him?

    VICTIM: Yes, they _____ him.

▶ **Practice 14. Simple past of irregular verbs.** (Chart 2-5)
Complete the sentences. Write the simple past of the irregular verbs in the list. Pay special attention to spelling. Use each verb only once.

✓ bite	catch	hold	pay	sting
blow	feel	mean	quit	swim

1. I broke a tooth when I _____*bit*_____ into a piece of hard candy.

2. The little boy _____ his mother's hand as they walked toward the school bus.

3. Maria promised to help us. I hope she _____ what she said.

4. Arthur _____ out all of the candles on his birthday cake.

5. We both _____ eating fried foods three months ago, and we already feel much better.

6. Douglas _____ the outside of his pocket to make sure his wallet was still there.

7. A bee _____ me on the hand while I was working in the garden.

8. Matthew Webb was the first person who _____ across the English Channel.

9. Paul _____ much more for his bike than I spent for mine.

10. Rita threw the ball high in the air. Daniel _____ it when it came down.

▶ **Practice 15. Simple past of irregular verbs.** (Chart 2-5)
Complete the sentences. Write the simple past form of the irregular verbs in the list. Pay special attention to spelling. Use each verb only once.

bet	freeze★	sink	split
choose	lead	✓ spend	upset
fly	ring	spin	weep

1. Dr. Perez _____spent_____ ten hours in the operating room performing delicate surgery.

2. On my first day at the university, my English teacher _____ the class to our classroom. We all followed him.

3. Sally and I made a friendly bet. I _____ her that my grade on the math test would be higher than hers.

4. I _____ when I heard the tragic news. Everyone else cried too.

5. As she got up, Lina _____ the table, and everything on top of it fell to the floor.

6. Paul wanted to make a fire, but the logs were too big. So he _____ them with his axe.

7. When I threw a piece of wood from the shore, it floated on top of the water. When I threw a rock, it _____ immediately to the bottom of the lake.

8. In 1927, Charles Lindbergh _____ from New York to Paris in 33 hours and 30 minutes.

9. When the children _____ around and around, they became dizzy.

10. The telephone _____ several times and then stopped before I could answer it.

11. William had trouble deciding which sweater he liked best, but he finally _____ the blue one.

12. The cold temperatures _____ the water in the pond, so we can go ice-skating today.

▶ **Practice 16. The simple past and the past progressive.** (Charts 2-7 and 2-8)
Complete the sentences. Write the correct form of the verbs in parentheses.

1. Maria (*call*) _____ me as soon as she got the good news.

2. Last night at about nine o'clock we (*watch*) _____ TV when someone knocked at the door.

3. During the study period in class yesterday, it was hard for me to concentrate because the student next to me (*hum*) _____ .

4. When Harry (*meet*) _____ Jenny, he immediately fell in love with her.

5. Jack was rushing to catch the bus when I (*see*) _____ him.

★*freeze* = stop moving completely.

6. Last Saturday while Sandy (*clean*) _____ out the attic, she found her grandmother's wedding dress.

7. It started to rain while I (*drive*) _____ to work this morning. I didn't have an umbrella with me. I (*get*) _____ very wet when I stepped out of my car.

8. When we looked outside during the storm, we saw that the wind (*blow*) _____ very hard, and the trees (*bend*) _____ over in the wind.

9. When the teacher came into the room, most of the children (*play*) _____ together nicely. But over in the corner, Bobby (*pull*) _____ Annie's hair. The teacher quickly ran over and pulled Bobby away from Annie.

▶ **Practice 17. The simple past and the past progressive.** (Charts 2-7 and 2-8)
Write "1" before the action that started first. Write "2" before the action that started second.

1. When the alarm clock rang, I was sleeping.

   _2_ The alarm clock rang.

   _1_ I was sleeping.

2. When I saw Dr. Jarvis yesterday evening, he was waving at me.

   ___ I saw Dr. Jarvis yesterday evening.

   ___ He was waving at me.

3. When I saw Dr. Jarvis yesterday evening, he waved at me.

   ___ I saw Dr. Jarvis yesterday evening.

   ___ He waved at me.

4. I closed the windows when it was raining.

   ___ I closed the windows.

   ___ It was raining.

5. I was closing the windows when it began to rain.

   ___ I was closing the windows.

   ___ It began to rain.

6. The server brought the check when we were eating our desserts.

   ___ The server brought the check.

   ___ We were eating our desserts.

7. When the doorbell rang, Sam went to the door. "Who is it?" he asked.

   ___ The doorbell rang.

   ___ Sam went to the door.

8. Sam was going to the door when the doorbell rang. "I'm coming, Bob," he said. "I saw you walking up the sidewalk."

   ___ The doorbell rang.

   ___ Sam was already going to the door.

► **Practice 18. The simple past and the past progressive.** (Charts 2-7 and 2-8)
Circle the correct form of the verbs in parentheses.

1. We (*had / were having*) a wonderful dinner last night to celebrate our 25th wedding anniversary.

2. We (*had / were having*) a wonderful time when suddenly the electric power went out.

3. When Richard (*stopped / was stopping*) his car suddenly, the groceries (*fell / were falling*) out of the grocery bags and (*spilled / were spilling*) all over the floor of the car.

4. When I was a child, my mother always (*served / was serving*) cookies and milk to my friends and me when they (*came / were coming*) home with me after school.

5. When we (*looked / were looking*) in on our baby last night, he (*slept / was sleeping*). I think he (*dreamt / was dreaming*) about something nice because he (*smiled / was smiling*).

6. A: Why is Henry in the hospital?

   B: He (*worked / was working*) on his car in the garage when the gas tank (*exploded / was exploding*).

   A: Oh! What (*caused / was causing*) the explosion?

   B: Henry (*dropped / was dropping*) a match too near the gas tank.

► **Practice 19. Simple present, present progressive, simple past, past progressive.** (Charts 2-1 → 2-4; 2-5, 2-7, and 2-8)
Underline the verbs. Decide which of the following phrases best describes the action of each sentence. Write the appropriate number.

1. actions occurring now or today
2. habitual / everyday actions
3. actions completed in the past (non-progressive)
4. one action in progress when another occurred

1. __2__ I take the bus to school when it rains.

2. __4__ I was riding the bus when I heard the news on my radio.

3. ____ I am riding the bus because my friend is repairing my bike.

4. ____ I rode the bus home yesterday because you forgot to pick me up.

5. ____ Dennis was having coffee this morning when a bird crashed into his kitchen window.

6. ____ Dennis had a big breakfast, but his wife didn't eat anything.

7. ____ Dennis is having a big breakfast this morning.

8. ____ Dennis generally has coffee with breakfast.

9. ____ My mother and I celebrate our birthdays together because they are just a few days apart.

10. ____ We were working when you called on our birthdays last week.

11. ____ One year we celebrated our birthdays apart because my mom was away on business.

► **Practice 20. Using progressive verbs with *always*.** (Chart 2-9)
Complete the dialogues. Write either the simple present or present progressive form of the verbs in the list and the given words in parentheses. If the speaker is expressing annoyance, use the present progressive.

✓ complain	leave	lose	study
interrupt	live	play	talk

1. A: Why won't you go out with Carlo anymore?
   B: He (*always*) _____*is always complaining*_____ about something. It was really irritating me to hear all those complaints!

2. A: How do you like your new roommate?
   B: I don't. He (*always*) _____ loudly on his phone. I can't have any peace and quiet in the room!

3. A: Why don't you come to our Friday night get-togethers, Al?
   B: I'd like to, but I _____ on the other side of town. It's too far.

4. A: Why are you so upset with Lisa?
   B: Oh, she (*forever*) _____ the towels on the bathroom floor. She never hangs them up.

5. A: What's the matter now? Why are you angry at me?
   B: Because you (*always*) _____ me! I never get a chance to finish a sentence!

6. A: Uh-oh. I can't find the keys to the car.
   B: Again? You (*always*) _____ them! You should tie them around your neck on a string.

7. A: What radio station do you listen to when you're in your car?
   B: I don't listen to the radio. I (*usually*) _____ my English lessons in the car. It's a good way to learn.

8. A: Sorry I can't join you tonight. I have to prepare for a test tomorrow.
   B: Oh, you (*always*) _____. Can't you take a break?

Complete the crossword puzzle. Use the clues under the puzzle. Write the correct form of the verbs in parentheses.

Across

2. Shhh. I'm (*listen*) _____ to the radio.

5. Good idea! I (*think*) _____ your suggestion is great.

7. What was that? I just (*hear*) _____ a loud noise.

8. I am (*think*) _____ about going home early today.

Down

1. We (*go*) _____ to Mexico last year.

3. I was in my room (*study*) _____ when you called.

4. I (*eat*) _____ lunch with friends yesterday.

6. This is fun. I'm (*have*) _____ a great time here.

7. I only (*have*) _____ a little money right now.

Chapter 3

Perfect and Perfect Progressive Tenses

▶ **Practice 1. Preview.** (Chapter 3)
Read the graph and the passage.

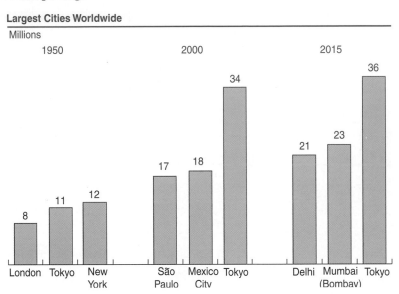

Largest Cities Worldwide

Source: United Nations, World Urbanization Projects: The 2003 Revision
(medium scenario), 2004. © 2006 Population Reference Bureau.

   Tokyo has been increasing in population since 1960. In fact, Tokyo has been the only city that has remained among the world's three largest cities since 1950. New York had once been the world's largest city. By the year 2000, it had dropped from the list. São Paulo and Mexico City were once among the largest cities too. Asian cities have been growing, and experts have estimated that in 2015, the three largest cities will be in Asia.

Part I. Look at the passage.

1. Write the three verbs in the present perfect tense.

   _____

2. Write the two verbs in the present perfect progressive tense.

   _____

3. Write the two verbs in the past perfect tense.

   _____

4. Write the one verb in the simple past tense.

   _____

5. Write the one verb in the future tense.

   _____

Part II. Circle "T" if the statement is true according to the graph and the passage, and "F" if it is false.

1. New York has been the largest city in the world since 1950.   T   F
2. Tokyo has been the largest city in the world for more than 50 years.   T   F
3. London had once been one of the three largest cities of the world.   T   F
4. In 1950, one city in India was one of the top three cities in world population. T   F
5. In 2015, two cities in India will be among the three largest cities of the world. T   F

▶ **Practice 2. The present perfect.** (Chart 3-1)
Complete the sentences using the present perfect tense. Write the correct past participle of the verbs in **bold**.

1. I often **eat** Thai food. I have _____ Thai food three times this week.
2. I sometimes **visit** my cousins on weekends. I have _____ them twice this month.
3. I **work** at the Regional Bank. I have _____ there for eleven years.
4. I **like** card games. I have _____ card games since I was a child.
5. I **know** Professor Blonsky. She's my next-door neighbor. I have _____ her all my life.
6. I **wear** glasses. I have _____ glasses since I was ten years old.
7. I **take** piano lessons. I have _____ piano lessons for several years.
8. I **go** to Unisex Haircutters once a month. I have _____ to the same shop for twenty years.
9. I **ride** a bicycle for exercise. I have _____ a bicycle for about twenty years.
10. I **am** in a bicycle-riding club. I have _____ a member of this club for fifteen years.

▶ **Practice 3. The present perfect.** (Chart 3-1)
Complete each sentence with *for* or *since*.

1. I haven't seen Elvira . . .
   a. _____ several years.
   b. _____ a long time.
   c. _____ the holiday last year.
   d. _____ she was in college.
   e. _____ more than a month.
   f. _____ she got married.
   g. _____ she became famous.

2. Mehdi and Pat have been friends . . .
   a. _____ they were in college.
   b. _____ about twenty years.
   c. _____ 1990.
   d. _____ a long time.
   e. _____ they began to work together.
   f. _____ they met.
   g. _____ their entire adult lives.

▶ **Practice 4. The present perfect.** (Chart 3-1)
Complete the sentences with the present perfect tense of the appropriate verb from the list. Use each verb only once. Include any words in parentheses.

> ✓ eat   know   ride   sweep   win
> improve   make   start   swim   write

1. A: How about more pie?

   B: No, but thanks. I can't swallow another bite. I (*already*) _____*have already eaten*_____
   too much.

2. Our football team is having a great season. They _____ all but one of their
   games so far this year and will probably win the championship.

3. Jane is expecting a letter from me, but I (*not*) _____ to her yet.
   Maybe I'll call her instead.

4. Jack is living in Spain now. His Spanish used to be terrible, but it _____
   greatly since he moved there.

5. A: Let's hurry! I think the movie is beginning!

   B: No, the movie (*not*) _____ yet. They're just showing previews of
   the coming attractions.

6. A: I hear your parents are coming to visit you. Is that why you're cleaning your apartment?

   B: You guessed it! I (*already*) _____ the floor, but I still need to
   dust the furniture. Want to help?

7. A: I understand Tom is a good friend of yours? How long (*you*) _____
   him?

   B: Since we were kids.

8. Everyone makes mistakes in life. I _____ lots of mistakes in my life. The
   important thing is to learn from one's mistakes. Right?

9. A: I (*never*) _____ on the subways in New York City. Have you?

   B: I've never even been to New York City.

10. A: (*you, ever*) _____ in the Atlantic Ocean?

    B: No, only the Pacific — when I was in Hawaii. I even went snorkeling when I was there.

► **Practice 5. The present perfect with *since*, *for*, and *ago*.** (Chart 3-1)
Complete the sentences with the correct time expression.

1. Today is _____the 21st of April_____. I started this job on April 1st. I started this job
   _____three weeks_____ ago. I have had this job since _____April 1st_____.
   I have had this job for _____three weeks_____.

2. I made a New Year's resolution on January 1st: I will get up at 6:00 A.M. every day instead of
   7:00 A.M. Today is March 1st, and I have gotten up every morning at 6:00 A.M. I made this
   resolution _____ ago. I have gotten up at 6:00 A.M. since
   _____. I have gotten up at 6:00 A.M. for
   _____.

3. Today is February 28th. Valentine's Day was on February 14th. I sent my girlfriend some
   chocolates on Valentine's Day, and she phoned to say "Thank you." After that, I did not hear
   from her again. I have not heard from her for _____. I have not
   heard from her since _____.

4. Today is October 27th, 2009. Sue works for Senator Brown. She began to work for him right
   after she first met him in October, 2000. She began to work for Senator Brown
   _____ ago. Sue has worked for Senator Brown for
   _____. She has worked for Senator Brown since
   _____.

► **Practice 6. The present perfect with *since* and *for*.** (Chart 3-1)
Rewrite the sentences using *since* and *for*.

1. We know Mrs. Jones. We met her last month.
   a. for _____We have known Mrs. Jones for one month._____
   b. since _____

2. They live in New Zealand. They moved there in 2001.
   a. for _____
   b. since _____

3. I like foreign films. I liked them five years ago.
   a. since _____
   b. for _____

4. Jack works for a software company. He started working there last year.
   a. for _____
   b. since _____

► **Practice 7. Is vs. has.** (Chart 3-2)
In spoken English, *is* and *has* can both be contracted to *'s*. Decide if the verb in the contraction is *is* or *has*.

Spoken English	**Written English**
1. He's absent.	*is*
2. Sue's been a nurse for a long time.	_____
3. Her brother's in the hospital.	_____
4. He's not happy.	_____
5. He's felt bad this past week.	_____
6. Here is a newspaper. Take one. It's free.	_____
7. The manager's taken some money.	_____
8. Mira's taking a break.	_____
9. Mira's taken a break.	_____

► **Practice 8. The present perfect and the simple past.** (Chart 3-3)
Circle the correct verb.

1. Botswana (*became / has become*) an independent country in 1966.

2. Botswana (*was / has been*) an independent country for more than 40 years.

3. It's raining. It (*was / has been*) raining since noon today.

4. It's raining. It's the rainy season. It (*rained / has rained*) every day since the first of the month.

5. I grew up in Scotland until I moved to Argentina with my family. I was 12 then. Now I am 21. I (*lived / have lived*) in Scotland for 12 years.

6. Now I live in Argentina. I (*lived / have lived*) in Argentina for 9 years.

7. Claude and Pierre worked together at the French restaurant for 30 years. They retired three years ago. They (*worked / have worked*) together for 30 years.

8. Claude and Pierre (*didn't work / haven't worked*) for the last three years.

► **Practice 9. The present perfect and the simple past.** (Chart 3-3)
Complete the sentences with the correct form of the verb in parentheses.

1. (*know*) I _____*knew*_____ Tim when he was a child, but I haven't seen him for many years. I _____*have known*_____ Larry, my best friend, for more than 20 years.

2. (*agree*) The company and the union finally _____ on salary raises two days ago. Since then, they _____ on everything, and the rest of the negotiations have gone smoothly.

3. (*take*) Mark _____ a trip to Asia last October. He _____ many trips to Asia since he started his own import-export business.

4. (*play*) Ivan _____ the violin at several concerts with the London Symphony since 1990. Last year he _____ Beethoven's violin concerto at one of the concerts.

5. (*write*) When she was in college, Julia _____ emails to her parents a few times a week. Now she has a job and is living in Chicago. In the last six months she _____ only three emails to her parents.

6. (*send*) Our university _____ 121 students to study in other countries last year. In total, we _____ 864 students abroad over the last ten years.

7. (*fly*) Masaru is a pilot for JAL. He _____ nearly 8 million miles during the last 22 years. Last year he _____ 380,000 miles.

8. (*oversleep*) Mark missed his physics examination this morning because he _____. He _____ a lot since the beginning of the semester. He'd better buy a new alarm clock.

▶ **Practice 10. The present perfect and the present perfect progressive.**
    (Charts 3-1 and 3-4)

Circle the correct verb.

1. Sam and Judy began talking on the phone at 9:00 P.M. Now it is 11:00 P.M., and they are still talking. They (*have talked / have been talking*) for two hours.

2. Sam and Judy speak to each other on the phone several times a day. They are speaking on the phone now, and they might speak again later. Today they (*have spoken / have been speaking*) to each other on the phone at least seven times.

3. England (*has won / has been winning*) the World Cup only once since 1930.

4. How long (*have you sat / have you been sitting*) here in the sun? You look like burnt toast! You'd better get out of the sun.

5. The chair in the president's office is very special. Sixteen presidents (*have sat / have been sitting*) in it.

▶ **Practice 11. The present perfect and the present perfect progressive.**
    (Charts 3-1 and 3-4)

Complete the sentences. Write either the present perfect or the present perfect progressive of the verbs in parentheses.

1. The children are at the park. They (*play*) ____have been playing____ ball for the last two hours, but they don't seem tired yet.

2. Jim (*play*) ____has played____ soccer only a couple of times, so he's not very good at it. He's much better at tennis.

3. Karl (*raise*) _____ three children to adulthood. Now they are educated and working in productive careers.

4. Sally is falling asleep at her desk. Dr. Wu (*lecture*) _____ since ten o'clock, and it's now past noon.

5. Jenna is a law student. Ever since she enrolled in law school, she (*miss, never*) _____ _____ a class due to illness.

6. Tim (*sleep*) _____ in the downstairs bedroom only once. He usually sleeps upstairs in the bedroom he shares with his brother.

7. A: How much longer until we arrive at the Singapore airport?

   B: Let me see. It's about 9:15. We (*fly*) _____ for almost six hours. We should be there in another couple of hours.

8. A: Janice (*sleep*) _____ for almost eleven hours. Don't you think we should wake her up?

   B: I guess we probably should.

9. A: Is the rescue crew still looking for survivors of the plane crash?

   B: Yes, they (*search*) _____ the area for hours, but they haven't found anybody else. They'll keep searching until nightfall.

▶ **Practice 12. The present perfect and the present perfect progressive.**
   (Charts 3-1 and 3-4)

Write the present perfect or the present perfect progressive of the verbs in the list. Use each verb only once. Include any words in parentheses.

| cook | hear | paint | stand | ✓ understand |
| grow | meet | spend | travel | want |

1. Bill and Mike have never gotten along with each other. I (*never*) _have never understood_ why they agreed to be roommates in the first place.

2. Al just introduced me to his sister. Now I _____ everyone in his family.

3. Ms. Erickson is a salesclerk in a large department store. It's almost closing time. Her feet hurt, as they do every day, because she _____ at the sales counter since eight o'clock this morning.

4. My uncle _____ the outside of his house for three weeks, and he's still not finished. He's being very careful. He wants his house to look just right.

5. I'm surprised that George apologized for what he said. As far as I can remember, I (*never*) _____ him say "I'm sorry" before.

6. The Smiths are presently in Tunisia. They _____ throughout North Africa since the middle of May. They'll return home in another month.

7. My brother's daughter _____ nearly six inches (15 cm) since I last saw her two years ago.

8. I have always _____ to travel abroad. Now the company I work for is going to send me on a sales trip to several countries.

9. A: How much money do you have to buy clothes with?

   B: Sixty dollars.

   A: I thought you had a hundred dollars.

   B: I did. But I (*already*) _____ forty.

10. A: Isn't the rice ready to eat yet? It _____ for over an hour,

    hasn't it? Are you sure you know how to cook rice?

    B: Of course I do! I've been watching the chefs on the cooking shows for years!

▶ **Practice 13. Simple past vs. the present perfect progressive.** (Charts 2-7 and 3-4)
Look at the information about Janet and write sentences with the given words. Use the simple past or present perfect progressive as necessary.

In 1998, Janet received her English teaching degree. Here is what happened to Janet after that:

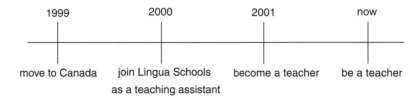

1999	2000	2001	now
move to Canada	join Lingua Schools as a teaching assistant	become a teacher	be a teacher

1. (move to Canada) _____*In 1999, Janet moved to Canada.*_____

2. (join Lingua Schools) _____

3. (live in Canada) _____

4. (be a teacher) _____

5. (teach her own class) _____

6. (work at Lingua Schools) _____

▶ **Practice 14. The simple past and the past perfect.** (Charts 2-6 and 3-5)
Underline each event. Write "1" over the event that happened first and "2" over the event that happened second.

           1   *2*
1. We had driven only two miles when we got a flat tire.

2. Alan told me that he had written a book.

3. By the time we arrived at the airport, the plane had already left.

4. The dog had eaten the entire roast before anyone knew it was gone.

5. We didn't stand in line for tickets because we had already bought them by mail.

6. Carl played the guitar so well because he had studied with a famous guitarist.

7. By the time the movie ended, everyone had fallen asleep.

8. After the professor had corrected the third paper, he was exhausted from writing comments on the students' papers.

9. I had just placed an order at the store for a new camera when I found a cheaper one online.

► **Practice 15. The past perfect.** (Chart 3-5)
Complete the sentences. Write the correct form of the past perfect.

1. Yesterday, John got 100% on a math exam. Before yesterday, he (*get, not*) _____ _____ 100%.

2. Last week, Sonya met her fiancé's parents. Before that, she (*meet, not*) _____ _____ them.

3. Today, Dan used a camera phone. Before today, he (*take, not*) _____ _____ pictures with one.

4. A few days ago, Bakir cooked a frozen dinner. Prior to that, he (*eat, not*) _____ _____ a frozen dinner.

5. Last week, I had to have a tooth pulled. Until then, I (*have, not*) _____ any problems with my teeth.

► **Practice 16. The simple past and the past perfect.** (Charts 2-7 and 3-5)
Complete the sentences with the simple past or past perfect form of the verb. Write the letter of the correct verb.

1. By the time Jason arrived to help, we _____ moving everything.
   a. already finished   b. had already finished

2. The apartment was hot when I got home, so I _____ the air conditioner.
   a. turned on   b. had turned on

3. The farmer's barn caught on fire some time during the night. By the time the firefighters arrived, the building _____ to the ground. It was a total loss.
   a. burned   b. had burned

4. The dinner I had at that restaurant was expensive! Until then, I _____ so much on one meal.
   a. never spent   b. had never spent

5. When I saw that Mike was having trouble, I _____ him. He was very appreciative.
   a. helped   b. had helped

6. My wife and I went to Disneyland when we visited Los Angeles last spring. Prior to that time, we _____ such a big amusement park. It was a lot of fun.
   a. never visited   b. had never visited

7. Last year I experienced how tedious long plane trips can be. I _____ on airplanes for fairly long distances before, but never as long as when I went to Australia in June.
   a. traveled   b. had traveled

► **Practice 17. The simple past and the past perfect.** (Charts 2-6 and 3-5)
Write the simple past or the past perfect of the verbs in parentheses. In some cases, both forms are correct.

1. Yesterday I (*go*) _____went_____ to my daughter's dance recital. I
   (*be, never*) _____had never been_____ to a dance recital before. I
   (*take, not*) _____didn't take_____ dancing lessons when I (*be*) _____was_____ a child.

2. Last night, I (*eat*) _____ four servings of food at the "all-you-can-eat" special dinner at The Village Restaurant. Until that time, I (*eat, never*) _____ so much in one meal. I've felt miserable all day today.

3. A: I (*see*) _____ you in the school play last night. You (*do*) _____ a terrific acting job. (*you, act, ever*) _____ in a play before this one?

   B: Yes. I (*start*) _____ acting when I was in elementary school.

▶ **Practice 18. The present perfect progressive and the past perfect progressive.** (Charts 3-4 and 3-7)

Circle the correct verb.

1. I'm studying English. I (*have been studying / had been studying*) English for several years now.

2. I came from Malaysia to live in New Zealand in 2002. I (*have been studying / had been studying*) English for three years before that.

3. Shhh! I want to see the end of this TV show! I (*have been waiting / had been waiting*) to find out who the murderer is.

4. Laura finally called me last night. I hadn't heard from her in four months. I (*have been waiting / had been waiting*) for that call for a long time!

5. Before Ada became a veterinarian last year, she (*has been working / had been working*) as a veterinarian's assistant while she was in school.

6. Li is going to quit his job. He (*has been working / had been working*) too many hours for too little money in this job. He is probably going to hand in his resignation next week.

▶ **Practice 19. The present perfect progressive and the past perfect progressive.** (Charts 3-4 and 3-7)

Complete the sentences. Write the present perfect progressive or the past perfect progressive form of the verbs in parentheses.

1. Anna (*listen*) _____had been listening_____ to loud rock music when her friends arrived, but she turned it off so all of them could study together. When they finished, she turned it back on, and now they (*dance*) _____have been dancing_____ and (*sing*) _____singing_____ for two hours.

2. We (*wait*) _____ for Ali for the last two hours, but he still hasn't arrived.

3. We (*wait*) _____ for Ali for over three hours before he finally arrived yesterday.

4. Oscar (*train*) _____ for the Olympics for the last three years and wants to make the national team next year.

5. The marathon runner (*run*) _____ for almost two hours when he collapsed to the pavement. He received immediate medical attention.

6. Tom had a hard time finding a job. He (try) _____ to get a new job for six months before he finally found a position at a local community college. Now he has a two-year contract. He (teach) _____ there for only a few weeks, but he likes his new job very much.

7. Dr. Sato (perform) _____ specialized surgery since she began working at the university hospital ten years ago. She still does many operations each year, but now her work is so famous that she travels all over the world lecturing to other surgeons on her technique.

8. The Acme Construction Company is having problems. They (work) _____ _____ on a new office building for the last seven months, and everything seems to be going wrong. Earlier, they stopped work on a smaller structure that they (build) _____ so they could take on this job. Now both projects are in jeopardy.

▶ **Practice 20. Chapter review.**
There is one verb error in each item. Correct the error.

1. *Citizen Kane* is a great classic movie. I've been seeing it ten times.

2. *War and Peace* is a long novel. I'm reading it for two months, and I am still not finished with it!

3. Our guests have left yesterday.

4. We were studying all night. Let's take a break now.

5. Let's not leave yet. I'd been having such a wonderful time at this party.

6. By the time I got home, the rest of the family has eaten.

7. I was late for my nine o'clock class, so I had run all the way from my dorm to my class.

8. Mrs. Wang isn't in the hospital anymore. She had left early this morning.

9. I was born on February 29th in 1960, a leap year. February 29th occurs only once every four years. So by the time the 21st century began, I celebrated only ten birthdays!

10. A: Are you still on the telephone? Are you holding on for someone?

    B: Yes, I am. I am still holding for the technical help department. I am holding for more than half an hour!

Chapter 4
Future Time

▶ **Practice 1. Simple future: *will.*** (Chart 4-1)
Correct the errors with ***will***. Two sentences have no errors.

1. Harry's birthday is tomorrow. He wills be fifty years old.

2. The store will stays open tomorrow night until 11:00 P.M.

3. Seventeen people will to be at the marketing meeting.

4. The new senator will make her first speech in Congress tomorrow.

5. Our teacher don't will be here tomorrow.

6. Will you call me tonight?

▶ **Practice 2. Simple future: *be going to.*** (Chart 4-1)
Complete the sentences with the correct form of ***be going to*** + the verb in parentheses.

1. Ben (*visit*) _____ his roommate's home for the holidays.

2. Delfina is a great tennis player. She (*win*) _____ the tennis
   tournament.

3. Which history course (*you, take*) _____ next semester?

4. The weather forecasters are saying it (*not, be*) _____ a
   cold winter this year.

5. What about Marta and Bob? (*they, join*) _____ us Saturday
   night?

6. I (*not, lie*) _____ to you. I (*tell*) _____
   _____ you the truth.

▶ **Practice 3. Simple future: *will* and *be going to.*** (Chart 4-1)

Complete the sentences in two ways. Write sentence a. with *will* and sentence b. with *be going to.* Use the correct verb from the list.

arrive	buy	rain	take
bloom	end	set	

1. a. The sun rose at 5:46 this morning, and it _____ at 6:52 tonight.

   b. The sun rose at 5:46 this morning, and it _____ at 6:52 tonight.

2. a. The flight left Bangkok at noon today, and it _____ in Mumbai at midnight.

   b. The flight left Bangkok at noon today, and it _____ in Mumbai at midnight.

3. a. There are dark clouds over the mountain. It _____ later today.

   b. There are dark clouds over the mountain. It _____ later today.

4. a. We planted the flowers in March, and they _____ in June.

   b. We planted the flowers in March, and they _____ in June.

5. a. Our semester began in January, and it _____ in May.

   b. Our semester began in January, and it _____ in May.

6. a. When _____ you _____ a new computer?

   b. When _____ you _____ a new computer?

7. a. I _____ not _____ a vacation this year. Maybe next year.

   b. I _____ not _____ a vacation this year. Maybe next year.

▶ **Practice 4. *Will* vs. *be going to.*** (Chart 4-2)

Read the sentences. Then check the box that describes the sentence.

		Prediction	**Prior Plan**	**Willingness**
1.	I'll help you change your tire, Ms. Olsen.			
2.	It's going to rain tomorrow.			
3.	It will rain tomorrow.			
4.	Louise is going to help us next week.			
5.	Wait. I'll help you carry your luggage.			
6.	We're going to see a movie tonight.			
7.	The moon will rise at 8:10 this evening.			

▶ **Practice 5. *Will* vs. *be going to.*** (Chart 4-2)
Circle a. if the meaning describes a prior plan. Circle b. if the meaning describes a decision of the moment.

1. I can't have lunch with you on Friday because I'm going to give a speech at noon to the Chamber of Commerce.
   a. prior plan   b. decision of the moment

2. My computer just crashed. I'll call the technical department to fix it right now.
   a. prior plan   b. decision of the moment

3. It's very icy and slippery on my street this morning. I'll go out and clear the sidewalk.
   a. prior plan   b. decision of the moment

4. Roberto and Sandy are going to get married next Saturday.
   a. prior plan   b. decision of the moment

5. Jimmy is going to have a tonsillectomy on Monday. The doctors are going to take out his tonsils because they are infected.
   a. prior plan   b. decision of the moment

6. Look at the price of the airport limo. It's too much money. We'll go to the airport by bus.
   a. prior plan   b. decision of the moment

▶ **Practice 6. *Will* vs. *be going to.*** (Chart 4-2)
Circle the correct response(s) to the questions or statements. More than one response may be correct.

1. A: What about Dominick? Doesn't he want to come with us?
   B: Nobody knows! (*I'll call him* / *I'm going to call him*) tonight to find out.

2. A: Jessica practices her violin for ten hours a day!
   B: I know! (*She's going to be* / *She'll be*) a famous violinist some day.

3. A: How about dinner and a movie on Friday?
   B: Sorry, I can't. (*I'm going to fly* / *I'll fly*) to London on Friday evening.

4. A: Do you and Paul have tickets for any of the hockey games this season?
   B: Yes, we do. (*We're going to the game* / *We'll go to the game*) tomorrow night.

5. A: I can't open this jar!
   B: Give it to me. (*I'm going to open it* / *I'll open it*) for you.

6. A: So you're leaving to go to another university, Professor Hu!
   B: Yes, (*I'm going to teach* / *I will teach*) at Emory University. They've made me a great offer.

▶ **Practice 7. *Will* vs. *be going to.*** (Chart 4-2)
Complete the sentences with *will* or *be going to* as appropriate. Include any words in parentheses.

1. A: Excuse me, waiter! This isn't what I ordered. I ordered a chicken salad.
   B: Sorry, sir. I _____*will*_____ take this back and get your salad.
   A: Thank you.

2. A: Would you like to join Linda and me tomorrow? We _____*are going to*_____ visit the natural history museum.
   B: Sure. I've never been there.

3. A: Where's the mustard?

   B: In the refrigerator, on the middle shelf.

   A: I've looked there.

   B: OK. I _____ get it for you.

4. A: What's all this paint for? (*you*) _____ paint your house?

   B: No, we _____ paint my mother's house.

5. A: Paul, do you want to go to the mall with me?

   B: No thanks. I already have plans. I _____ wash my car and then clean
   out the basement.

6. A: Someone needs to take this report to Mr. Day's office right away, but I can't leave my desk.

   B: I _____ do it.

   A: Thanks.

7. A: Who'll pick up Uncle Jack at the airport?

   B: I _____.

8. A: Why is Carlos wearing a suit and tie? He usually wears jeans to class.

   B: He _____ give a speech at the faculty lunch today.

9. A: Let me ask you something, Toshi.

   B: Sure. What's up, Andy?

   A: I _____ interview for a job this afternoon, and . . . well, do I need
   a tie? I don't have a decent one!

   B: Yes, you need a tie. I _____ lend you one of mine.

   A: Thanks.

10. A: You're going out?

    B: Yes. I _____ stop at the grocery store for some fruit and some
    rice. Can you think of anything else we need?

    A: How about getting some chocolate-covered nuts?

    B: Good idea! I _____ get some of those too.

▶ **Practice 8. Expressing the future in time clauses.** (Chart 4-3)
Underline the time clause in each sentence and circle its verb.

1. I'll see you when you (return) from your trip.

2. After the rain stops, we'll go out.

3. We're going to keep driving until it gets dark.

4. As soon as the baby is born, we'll let you know!

5. When he retires, Barry is going to take painting classes.

6. You will be able to vote when you are eighteen years old.

7. I'm going to go to bed as soon as the late news is over.

8. The students will return to campus when the new semester begins.

▶ **Practice 9. Expressing the future in time clauses.** (Chart 4-3)
Complete the sentences with the correct form of the verb.

1. Grandma and Grandpa are planning to travel often when they (*retire*) _____.

2. I'll wake up tomorrow morning when the alarm clock (*ring*) _____.

3. The students will relax after they (*finish*) _____ their final exams.

4. You'll feel a lot better after you (*take*) _____ this medicine.

5. The residents of the coastal areas will prepare for the hurricane before it
   (*arrive*) _____.

6. Mark will work in a law firm as soon as he (*graduate*) _____ from law
   school.

7. We'll have dinner as soon as the rice (*be*) _____ ready.

8. I'll tell you as soon I (*hear*) _____ any news.

9. Before we (*leave*) _____ on vacation, we'll stop our newspaper delivery.

10. We'll start our newspaper delivery again after we (*get*) _____ back from vacation.

▶ **Practice 10. Expressing the future in time clauses.** (Chart 4-3)
Write the letter of the clause from either Column A or Column B to complete the sentences
correctly.

	Column A	Column B
1. When I see Irina later, _b_.	a. I give her the news	b. I'll give her the news
2. I'll call you tomorrow _____.	a. after I talk to Rita	b. after I will talk to Rita
3. As soon as I hear from Tom, _____.	a. I call you	b. I'll call you
4. We'll all be very happy _____.	a. when you get here	b. when you will get here
5. I'll save my files _____.	a. before I shut down my computer	b. before I will shut down my computer
6. The passengers will get off the plane _____.	a. after it lands	b. after it is going to land
7. My cell phone won't work _____.	a. until I unlock it	b. until I will unlock it
8. After the party is over tonight, _____.	a. we call a taxi to go home	b. we'll call a taxi to go home
9. I'm not going to pay for the refrigerator _____.	a. until they fix the broken door	b. until they will fix the broken door
10. I'll take this new medicine _____.	a. before I go to bed tonight	b. before I will go to bed tonight

► **Practice 11. Expressing the future in time clauses.** (Chart 4-3)
Complete the sentences with the following: the simple present, the future with **will**, or the future with a form of **be going to**. In some sentences, both **will** and **be going to** may be possible.

1. The strike has been going on for over two months now. The strikers

   (*return, not*) _____will not / are not going to return_____ to work until they (*get*) _____get_____

   a raise and the benefits they are demanding.

2. When Rita (*get*) _____ her driver's license next week, she (*be*) _____

   _____ able to drive to school every day.

3. A: Mr. Jackson called. He'll be here at the garage to pick up his car in a few minutes. He

      (*be, not*) _____ very happy when he (*learn*) _____ about

      the bill for repairs on his car. Do you want to talk to him when he (*come*) _____

      in and (*ask*) _____ about his bill?

   B: Not especially, but I will.

4. After Ali (*return*) _____ to his country next month, he (*start*) _____

   _____ working at the Ministry of Agriculture.

5. According to the newspaper, the Department of Transportation (*build*) _____

   _____ a new four-lane highway into the city next year. In my opinion, it

   (*be*) _____ obsolete before they (*complete*) _____ it.

   It seems to me that a six-lane highway is needed to handle the heavy traffic.

6. A: Have you heard any news about Barbara since her car accident?

   B: No, I've heard nothing. As soon as I (*hear*) _____ something, I

      (*let*) _____ you know.

7. A: I see you're reading *The Silk Road*.

   B: I (*lend*) _____ it to you as soon as I (*finish*) _____ it.

   A: Really? Thanks!

8. A: Relax. The plumber is on his way. He (*be*) _____ here before

      long to fix that leak in the pipe under the kitchen sink.

   B: Oh, good. I (*be*) _____ happy to get that pipe fixed.

▶ **Practice 12. Using the present progressive and the simple present to express future time.** (Chart 4-4)

Complete the second sentence with a form of the present progressive to express the same meaning as the first sentence.

1. I'm going to see the dentist tomorrow.

   I _____ the dentist tomorrow.

2. She will have a baby in July.

   She _____ a baby in July.

3. The new store will open in September.

   The new store _____ in September.

4. The office staff is going to work late tonight.

   The office staff _____ late tonight.

5. We're going to have a graduation party for Miriam on Saturday.

   We _____ a graduation party for Miriam on Saturday.

6. Shelley and Sue are going to attend the conference in New York next April.

   Shelley and Sue _____ the conference in New York next April.

▶ **Practice 13. Using the present progressive and the simple present to express future time.** (Chart 4-4)

Circle the letter of the phrases which can complete the sentences correctly. More than one completion may be correct for each sentence.

1. We have tickets for a puppet show today. The show _____.
   a. starts at 2:00 P.M.
   b. is starting at 2:00 P.M.
   c. is going to start at 2:00 P.M.

2. Look at those black clouds! Pretty soon it _____.
   a. rains
   b. is raining
   c. is going to rain

3. This afternoon I have a lunch date with a friend. After that, we _____.
   a. are going to visit her aunt
   b. are visiting her aunt
   c. visit her aunt

4. I'm hurrying to catch a plane. It _____!
   a. leaves in an hour
   b. is going to leave in an hour
   c. is leaving in an hour

5. Sorry I can't meet with you tomorrow, Helen. I have an important appointment. _____ with the president at noon.
   a. I'm meeting
   b. I'm going to meet
   c. I will meet

6. A: Nobody has volunteered to bring the drinks for the festival Saturday night. Olga, how about you? Harry, how about you? Please . . . can somebody help us out?

   B: OK, OK. _____ it.

   a. I'll do
   b. I'm doing
   c. I'm going to do

▶ **Practice 14. Using the present progressive to express future time.** (Chart 4-4)
Change the verbs in *italics* to a form of the present progressive in the sentences that express a planned event or definite intention. For the sentences where no change is possible, write "NC."

1. A: The package has to be there tomorrow. Will it get there in time?

   B: Don't worry. *I'm going to send* it by express mail.

      ___*I'm sending it by express mail.*_____

2. A: What's the weather report?

   B: *It is going to rain* tomorrow morning.

      ___*NC*_____

3. A: Would you like to have dinner with me tonight, Pat?

   B: Thanks, but *I'm going to have* dinner with my sister and her husband.

      _____

4. A: What *are you going to do* this evening?

   B: *I'm going to study* at the library.

      _____

      _____

5. A: Oh, I spilled my coffee on the floor.

   B: *I'll help* you clean it up.

      _____

6. A: Did you know that Kathy and Paul are engaged?

   B: No. That's great! When *are they going to get* married?

   A: In September.

      _____

7. A: *You're going to laugh* when I tell you what happened to me today!

   B: Oh? What happened?

      _____

8. A: Have you lived here long?

   B: No, not long. Only about a year. But *we're going to move* again next month. My father's company has reassigned him to Atlanta, Georgia.

      _____

9. A: I tried to register for Professor Stein's economics class, but it's full. *Is he going to teach* it again next semester?

   B: I think so.

   _____

10. A: Son, *I'm not going to send* you any money this month. You're spending far too much. You need to learn to be more careful.

    _____

    B: But Dad . . . !

    A: Just do the best you can. *I am going to come* to visit you next month. We can talk about it then.

    _____

▶ **Practice 15. Future progressive.** (Chart 4-5)
Complete the sentences. Write the future progressive form of the verbs in **bold**.

1. Every night at 7:00 I **sit** down **to have** dinner. Tomorrow at 7:10, I

   _____ dinner.

2. We **fly** to Italy tomorrow night. Tomorrow night at this time, we

   _____ over the Atlantic Ocean.

3. On Sunday mornings, I **sleep** late. Next Sunday morning at 9:00 A.M., I

   _____ .

4. It always **snows** in December in Moscow. We're going to Moscow in December. At that time,

   it _____ in Moscow.

5. Ellen always **watches** late movies on TV. I'm sure that tonight she

   _____ an old movie on TV around 2:00 A.M.

▶ **Practice 16. Future progressive.** (Charts 4-3 and 4-5)
Complete the sentences with the future progressive or the simple present form of the verbs in parentheses.

1. Just relax, Antoine. As soon as your sprained ankle (*heal*) _____heals_____, you can play soccer again. At this time next week, you (*play*) ____will be playing____ soccer again.

2. I'll meet you at the airport tomorrow. After you (*clear*) _____ customs, look for me just outside the gate. I (*stand*) _____ right by the door.

3. Ingrid and Ruth won't be at this school when classes (*start*) _____ next semester. They (*attend*) _____ a new school in Taiwan.

4. Please come and visit today when you (*have*) _____ a chance. I

   (*shop*) _____ from 1:00 to about 3:00, but I'll be home after that.

5. I won't be here next week, students. I (*attend*) _____ a seminar in Los Angeles. Ms. Gomez will be the substitute teacher. When I (*return*) _____, I will expect you to be ready for the midterm examination.

► **Practice 17. Future perfect and future perfect progressive.** (Chart 4-6)
Complete the sentences with the future perfect or the future perfect progressive form of the verbs in the list. Include any words in parentheses. Use each verb only once.

> | | | | |
> |---|---|---|---|
> | drink | land | ride | save |
> | fly | listen | ✓ rise | teach |

1. By the time I get up tomorrow morning, the sun (*already*) _____*will already have risen*_____.

2. This is a long trip! By the time we get to Miami, we _____ on this bus for over 15 hours.

3. We're going to be late meeting my brother's plane. By the time we get to the airport, it (*already*) _____.

4. He's never going to stop talking. In 15 more minutes, we _____ to him lecture for three solid hours. I don't even know what he's saying anymore.

5. I drink too much coffee. I have already had two cups this morning, and I will probably have two more cups. This means that before lunch, I _____ four cups of coffee.

6. This is the longest flight I have ever taken. By the time we get to New Zealand, we _____ for 13 hours. I'm going to be exhausted.

7. Douglas has been putting some money away every month to prepare for his trip to South America next year. By the end of this year, he _____ enough.

8. Can you believe it? According to our grammar teacher, by the end of this semester, she _____ more than 3,000 students from 42 different countries. She has been teaching for nearly 20 years — and she still loves it!

► **Practice 18. Chapter review.**
These sentences describe typical events in a day in the life of a woman named Kathy. The sentences are in the past, but all of these things will happen in Kathy's life tomorrow. Change all of the sentences to the future. Use **will**.

1. When Kathy got up yesterday morning, the sun was shining. The same thing will happen tomorrow. When Kathy _____*gets*_____ up tomorrow morning, the sun _____*will be shining*_____.

2. Yesterday she brushed her teeth and showered. Then she made a light breakfast. Tomorrow will be the same. She _____ her teeth and _____. Then she _____ a light breakfast.

3. After she ate breakfast yesterday, she got ready to go to work. And tomorrow after she _____ breakfast, she _____ ready to go to work.

4. By the time she got to work yesterday, she had drunk three cups of coffee. Tomorrow she'll do the same. By the time she _____ to work, she _____ three cups of coffee.

5. Between 8:00 and 9:00, Kathy answered her email and planned her day. She has the same plans for tomorrow. Between 8:00 and 9:00, Kathy _____ her e-mail and _____ her day.

6. By 10:00 yesterday, she had called three new clients. Tomorrow, by 10:00, she _____ three new clients.

7. At 11:00 yesterday, she was attending a staff meeting. She plans to do the same tomorrow. At 11:00, she _____ a staff meeting.

8. She went to lunch at noon and had a sandwich and a bowl of soup. Tomorrow she _____ to lunch at noon and _____ a sandwich and a bowl of soup.

9. After she finished eating, she took a short walk in the park before she returned to the office. Tomorrow she'll do the same. After she _____ eating, she _____ a walk in the park before she _____ to the office.

10. She worked at her desk until she went to another meeting in the middle of the afternoon. And tomorrow she _____ at her desk until she _____ to another meeting in the middle of the afternoon.

11. By the time she left the office, she had attended three meetings. Tomorrow she'll follow the same schedule. By the time she _____ the office, she _____ three meetings.

12. When Kathy got home, her children were playing in the yard, and Grandma was watching them from the porch. Tomorrow will be the same. When Kathy _____ home, her children _____ in the yard, and Grandma _____ them from the porch.

13. The children had been playing since 3:00 in the afternoon. And tomorrow they _____ since 3:00 in the afternoon.

14. The family had dinner together and talked about their day. Tomorrow will be the same. They _____ dinner together, and they _____ about their day.

15. They watched television for a while, and then Kathy and her husband put the kids to bed. The same thing will happen tomorrow. They _____ television for a while, and then they _____ the kids to bed.

16. By the time Kathy went to bed yesterday, she had had a full day and was ready for sleep. Tomorrow will be the same for Kathy. By the time she _____ to bed, she _____ a full day and _____ ready for sleep.

Chapter 5
Review of Verb Tenses

▶ **Practice 1. Verb tense review.** (Chapters 1 → 4)
Circle the correct verb.

1. My grandfather (*has never flown* / *had never flown*) in an airplane, and he has no intention of ever doing so.

2. Jane isn't here yet. I (*am waiting* / *have been waiting*) for her since noon, but she still (*didn't arrive* / *hasn't arrived*).

3. In all the world, there (*have been* / *are*) only 14 mountains that (*reach* / *are reaching*) above 8,000 meters (26,247 feet).

4. When my parents were teenagers, people (*hadn't owned* / *didn't own*) computers. By the time I was a teenager, I (*was owning* / *had owned*) a computer for several years.

5. Right now we (*are having* / *have*) a heat wave. The temperature (*is* / *has been*) in the upper 90s Fahrenheit (30s Celsius) for the last six days.

6. I have a long trip ahead of me tomorrow, so I think I'd better go to bed. Let me say good-bye now because I won't see you in the morning. I (*will leave* / *will have left*) by the time you (*get* / *will get*) up.

7. Last night I (*went* / *was going*) to a party. When I (*get* / *got*) there, the room was full of people. Some of them (*danced* / *were dancing*) and others (*talked* / *were talking*). One young woman (*was standing* / *has been standing*) by herself. I (*have never met* / *had never met*) her before, so I (*introduced* / *was introducing*) myself to her.

8. About three o'clock yesterday afternoon, Jessica (*was sitting* / *had sat*) in bed reading a book. Suddenly, she (*heard* / *was hearing*) a loud noise and (*got* / *was getting*) up to see what it was. She (*has looked* / *looked*) out the window. A truck (*has just backed* / *had just backed*) into her new car!

▶ **Practice 2. Verb tense review.** (Chapters 1 → 4)
Circle the correct verb.

1. Next month I have a week's vacation. I (*take* / *am taking*) a trip. I (*leave* / *left*) on Saturday, July 2nd. First, I (*'ve gone* / *'m going*) to Madison, Wisconsin, to visit my brother. After I (*will leave* / *leave*) Madison, I (*am going to go* / *have gone*) to Chicago to see a friend who (*is studying* / *will have studied*) at the university there. She (*has lived* / *lives*) in Chicago for three years, so she (*knows* / *knew*) her way around the city. She (*has promised* / *will be promising*) to take me to many interesting places. I (*had never been* / *have never been*) to Chicago, so I (*am looking* / *have looked*) forward to going there.

2. The weather is beautiful today, but until this morning, it (*has been raining / had been raining*) steadily for almost a week. A week ago, the temperature suddenly (*was dropping / dropped*), and after that we had bad weather for a week. Now the weather forecaster says that tomorrow it (*is going to be / is*) very warm. The weather certainly (*was changing / changes*) quickly here. I never know what to expect. Who knows? When I (*wake / will wake*) up tomorrow morning, maybe it (*snows / will be snowing*).

▶ **Practice 3. Verb tense review.** (Chapters 1 → 4)
Complete the sentences with the verbs in parentheses. Use any appropriate tense.

On June 20th, I returned home. I (*be*) _____ away from home for two years. My
                                              1
family (*meet*) _____ me at the airport with kisses and tears. They (*miss*) _____
                       2   3
me as much as I had missed them. I (*be*) _____ very happy to see them again.
                                                  4

When I (*get*) _____ the chance, I (*take*) _____ a long look at them. My
                     5   6
little brother (*be*) _____ no longer little. He (*grow*) _____ a lot. He
                             7   8
(*be*) _____ almost as tall as my father. My little sister (*wear*) _____
              9   10
a green dress. She (*change*) _____ quite a bit too, but she
                                       11
(*be, still*) _____ mischievous and inquisitive. She (*ask*) _____
                     12   13
me a thousand questions a minute, or so it seemed.

My father (*gain*) _____ some weight, and his hair (*turn*) _____
                           14   15
a little grayer, but otherwise he was just as I had remembered him. My mother

(*look*) _____ a little older, but not much. The wrinkles on her face
                16
(*be*) _____ smile wrinkles.
              17

▶ **Practice 4. Verb tense review.** (Chapters 1 → 4)
Complete the sentences with the verbs in parentheses. Use any appropriate tense.

On June 20th, I will return home. I (*be*) _____ away from home for
                                                   1
two years by that time. My family (*meet*) _____ me at the airport with kisses and
                                                   2
tears. They (*miss*) _____ me as much as I have missed them. I
                            3
(*be*) _____ very happy to see them again.
              4
When I (*get*) _____ a chance, I (*take*) _____ a long look at them. My
                     5   6
little brother (*be, no longer*) _____ so little. He (*grow*) _____
                                        7   8
at least a foot. He (*be*) _____ almost as tall as my father. My little sister
                                  9
(*wear, probably*) _____ a green dress because that's her favorite color.
                           10
She (*change*) _____ quite a bit too, but she
                       11

(*be, still*) _____ mischievous and inquisitive. She (*ask*) _____ me a
                    12   13
thousand questions a minute, or so it will seem.

My father (*gain, probably*) _____ some weight, and his hair
                                              14
(*turn*) _____ a little grayer, but otherwise he will be just as I remember
              15
him. My mother (*look*) _____ a little older, but not much. The wrinkles on her face
                               16
(*be*) _____ smile wrinkles.
           17

▶ **Practice 5. Verb tense review.** (Chapters 1 → 4)
Complete the sentences in each part with verbs from the list. Use any appropriate tense.

Part I.

| be | break | do | happen | have | play | recuperate | see |

A: Where's Sonia? I (*not*) _____ her lately.
                                        1

B: She's at home _____ from an accident.
                          2

A: An accident? What _____ to her?
                                3

B: She _____ her arm while she _____ volleyball last week in the
              4   5
game against South City College.

A: Gosh, that's too bad. I'm sorry to hear that. How _____ she _____?
                                                              6   7

B: OK, I guess. Actually, she _____ a cast on her arm, but she is not in any pain. I
                                        8
think that she _____ back in class next week.
                        9

Part II.

A: Hello. Computer Data Magazine. How can I help you?

B: Well, I _____ in my money for a subscription to your magazine, *Computer Data,* two
   ₁

months ago, but to date I (*not*) _____ any issues.
   ₂

A: I'm sorry to hear that. Unfortunately, one of our main computers (*not*) _____
   ₃

_____ at the moment. However, our computer specialists

_____ very hard to fix it at the present time. Your new subscription
   ₄

_____ as soon as possible.
   ₅

B: Thank you.

▶ **Practice 6. Verb tense review.** (Chapters 1 → 4)
Complete the sentences with the verbs in parentheses. Use any appropriate tense.

A: Have you ever heard of the Socratic method?

B: No, I haven't. What is it?

A: It's a method of teaching that Socrates (*use*) _____ in ancient Greece more
   ₁

than two thousand years ago. Some teachers still (*use*) _____ this kind of
   ₂

method today.

B: Really? What (*it, consist*) _____ of today? How
   ₃

(*teachers, use*) _____ this method now?
   ₄

A: Well, the teacher (*not, give*) _____ any information to the students. She
   ₅

or he just asks a series of questions, but (*not, make*) _____ any
   ₆

statements. The teacher (*know*) _____ what the important questions to ask the
   ₇

students are. Then the students have to think about the answers.

B: That (*sound*) _____ good to me! When I was in high school, I had a lot of
   ₈

teachers who just (*talk*) _____ too much. Sometimes the students even
   ₉

(*fall*) _____ asleep in class!
   ₁₀

A: I (*agree*) _____ with you. You will learn faster after you
   ₁₁

(*think*) _____ about something than if you just have to remember facts.
   ₁₂

B: That's true. I (*take*) _____ a philosophy class now with a wonderful
    13

professor. She (*always, ask*) _____ questions! I guess she
                                    14

(*use*) _____ the Socratic method for the whole semester, and I
            15

(*not, realize*) _____ it !
                    16

▶ **Practice 7. Verb tense review.** (Chapters 1 → 4)
Complete the sentences with the correct form of the verb in parentheses.

1. Nora is at the hospital because her cousin is having surgery today. The surgery began at 7:00
    and is expected to end at noon. Nora arrived at the hospital at 8:00 A.M.

    a. It's 8:10 A.M. Nora (*wait*) _____ in the waiting room.

    b. It is now 9:00 A.M. Nora (*wait*) _____ for one hour.

    c. By 11:00, the surgery will still be going on, and Nora will still be waiting in the waiting
        room. At that time, Nora (*wait*) _____ in the waiting room
        for three hours.

2. Hundreds of passengers are in the security line at the airport. Jaime entered the security line at
    8:00 A.M.

    a. It's 8:15 A.M. Jaime (*stand*) _____ in the security line at the airport.

    b. It is now 9:00 A.M. Jaime (*stand*) _____ in the security line
        for an hour.

    c. Jaime is probably going to be standing in the security line for another hour. By 9:30 A.M.,
        he (*stand*) _____ in the security line for an hour and a half.

    d. Jaime is probably going to be finished standing in the security line by 10:00 A.M. If he is
        finished at 10:00 A.M., he (*stand*) _____ in line for a total of two
        hours!

▶ **Practice 8. Verb tense review.** (Chapters 1 → 4)
Complete the sentences. Write the letter of the correct completion.

1. A: Hurry up! We're waiting for you. What's taking you so long?

    B: I ____ for an important phone call. Go ahead and leave without me.
        a. wait   c. have waited
        b. will have waited   d. am waiting

2. A: Robert is going to be famous someday. He ____ in three movies already.

    B: I'm sure he'll be a star.
        a. has been appearing   c. has appeared
        b. had appeared   d. appeared

3. A: Where's Polly?

    B: She ____.
        a. is in her room studying   c. studies in her room
        b. in her room is studying   d. has studied in her room

4. A: What _____ of the new simplified tax law?

   B: It's more confusing than the old one.
   a. are you thinking   c. have you thought
   b. do you think   d. have you been thinking

5. A: When is Mr. Fields planning to retire?

   B: Soon, I think. He _____ here for a long time. He'll probably retire either next year or the
      year after that.
   a. worked   c. has been working
   b. had been working   d. is working

6. A: Why did you buy all this sugar and chocolate?

   B: I _____ a delicious chocolate cake for dinner tonight.
   a. make   c. 'm going to make
   b. will make   d. will have made

7. A: Let's go! What's taking you so long?

   B: I'll be there as soon as I _____ my keys.
   a. find   c. 'm going to find
   b. will find   d. am finding

8. Next week when there _____ a full moon, the ocean tides will be higher.
   a. is being   c. is
   b. will be   d. will have been

9. While I _____ TV last night, a mouse ran across the floor.
   a. have watched   c. watched
   b. was watching   d. have been watching

10. Fish were among the earliest forms of life. Fish _____ on earth for ages and ages.
    a. existed   c. exist
    b. are existing   d. have existed

11. The phone _____ constantly since Jack announced his candidacy for president this morning.
    a. has been ringing   c. had rung
    b. rang   d. had been ringing

12. The earth _____ on the sun for its heat and light.
    a. depended   c. was depending
    b. depending   d. depends

13. I don't feel good. I _____ home from work tomorrow.
    a. 'm staying   c. stay
    b. will have stayed   d. stayed

14. Today there are weather satellites that beam down information about the earth's atmosphere.
    In the last several decades, space exploration _____ great contributions to weather forecasting.
    a. is making   c. makes
    b. has made   d. made

15. On July 20th, 1969, astronaut Neil Armstrong _____ down onto the moon. He was the first person ever to set foot on another celestial body.
    a. was stepping
           c. stepped
    b. has stepped
           d. has been stepping

16. The plane's departure was delayed because of mechanical difficulties. When the weary passengers finally boarded the aircraft, many were annoyed and irritable because they _____ in the airport for three and a half hours.
    a. are waiting
           c. have been waiting
    b. were waiting
           d. had been waiting

17. If coastal erosion continues to take place at the present rate, in another fifty years this beach _____ anymore.
    a. doesn't exist
           c. isn't existing
    b. isn't going to exist
           d. won't be existing

18. Homestead High School's football team _____ a championship until last season when the new coach led them to win first place in their league.
    a. has never won
           c. had never been winning
    b. is never winning
           d. had never won

19. Nonnative speakers need many years of intensive language study before they can qualify as interpreters. By the end of this year, Chen _____ English for three years, but he will still need more training and experience before he masters the language.
    a. will be studying
           c. will have been studying
    b. has studied
           d. has been studying

▶ **Practice 9. Verb tense review.** (Chapters 1 → 4)
Complete the sentences. Write the letter of the correct completion.

1. A: May I speak to Dr. Paine, please?

   B: I'm sorry, he _____ a patient at the moment. Can I help you?
    a. is seeing
           c. was seeing
    b. sees
           d. has been seeing

2. A: When are you going to ask your boss for a raise?

   B: _____ to her twice already! I don't think she wants to give me one.
    a. I've talked
           c. I've been talking
    b. I was talking
           d. I'd talked

3. A: Do you think Harry will want something to eat after he gets here?

   B: I hope not. It'll probably be after midnight, and we _____.
    a. are sleeping
           c. have been sleeping
    b. will be sleeping
           d. be sleeping

4. Paul, could you please turn off the stove? The potatoes _____ for at least 30 minutes.
    a. are boiling
           c. have been boiling
    b. boiling
           d. were boiling

5. A: Is it true that spaghetti didn't originate in Italy?

   B: Yes. The Chinese _____ spaghetti dishes for a long time before Marco Polo brought it back
      to Italy.
      a. have been making   c. had been making
      b. have made   d. make

6. A: I once saw a turtle that had wings. The turtle flew into the air to catch insects.

   B: Stop kidding. I _____ you!
      a. don't believe   c. didn't believe
      b. am not believing   d. wasn't believing

7. A: Could someone help me lift the lawnmower into the pickup truck?

   B: I'm not busy. I _____ you.
      a. help   c. am helping
      b. 'll help   d. am going to help

8. My family loves this house. It _____ the family home ever since my grandfather built it 60
   years ago.
      a. was   c. will be
      b. has been   d. is

9. Here's an interesting statistic: On a typical day, the average person _____ about 48,000 words.
   How many words did you speak today?
      a. spoke   c. is speaking
      b. was speaking   d. speaks

10. It's against the law to kill the black rhinoceros. They _____ extinct.
      a. became   c. are becoming
      b. have become   d. become

11. After ten unhappy years, Janice finally quit her job. She _____ along with her boss for a long
    time before she finally decided to look for a new position.
      a. hadn't been getting   c. didn't get
      b. isn't getting   d. hasn't been getting

12. The National Hurricane Center is closely watching a strong hurricane over the Atlantic Ocean.
    When it _____ the coast of Texas sometime tomorrow afternoon, it will bring with it great
    destructive force.
      a. reaches   c. reaching
      b. will reach   d. is reaching

13. At one time, huge prehistoric reptiles dominated the earth. This Age of Dinosaurs _____ much
    longer than the present Age of Mammals has lasted to date.
      a. lasted   c. had lasted
      b. was lasting   d. has lasted

14. Jim, why don't you take some time off? You _____ too hard lately. Take a short vacation.
      a. worked   c. have been working
      b. work   d. were working

15. The city is rebuilding its dilapidated waterfront, transforming it into a pleasant and fashionable outdoor mall. Next summer when the tourists arrive, they _____ 104 beautiful new shops and restaurants in the area where the old run-down waterfront properties used to stand.
      a. will found   c. will find
      b. will be finding   d. will have found

16. A minor earthquake occurred at 2:07 A.M. on January 3rd. Most of the people in the village _____ at the time and didn't even know it had occurred until the next morning.
      a. slept   c. sleep
      b. had slept   d. were sleeping

17. The little girl started to cry. She _____ her doll, and no one was able to find it for her.
      a. has lost   c. was lost
      b. had lost   d. was losing

18. According to research, people usually _____ in their sleep 25 to 30 times each night.
      a. turn   c. turned
      b. are turning   d. have turned

Chapter 6
Subject-Verb Agreement

▶ **Practice 1. Preview.** (Chapter 6)
Correct the errors in the use of singular and plural forms of nouns and verbs. Don't add any new words.

1. My mother wear_∧ glasses. *(s inserted above with caret)*

2. Elephants is large animals.

3. Your heart beat faster when you exercise.

4. Healthy hearts needs regular exercise.

5. Every child in the class know the alphabet.

6. Some of the magazine at the dentist's office are two year old.

7. A number of the students in my class is from Mexico.

8. One of my favorite subject in school is algebra.

9. There's many different kind of insects in the world.

10. Writing compositions are difficult for me.

11. The United States have a population of over 300 million.

12. Most of the movie take place in Paris.

13. Most of the people in my factory division likes and gets along with one another, but a few of the worker doesn't fit in with the rest of us very well.

► **Practice 2. Final -s on nouns and verbs.** (Chart 6-1)
Look at the words that end in **-s**. Are they nouns or verbs? Are they singular or plural? Check the correct columns.

	Noun	Verb	Singular	Plural
1. A boat floats.		✓	✓	
2. Boats float.				
3. My friend lives in my neighborhood.				
4. My friends live in my neighborhood.				
5. Helen eats a cookie every morning.				
6. Donuts contain a lot of sugar.				
7. Babies cry when they are hungry.				
8. My baby cries every night.				

► **Practice 3. Pronunciation and spelling of final -s/-es.** (Chart 6-1)
Add **-s** or **-es** to these words to spell them correctly. Then write /s/, /z/, or /əz/ to show the pronunciation of the endings.

1. ball ___s___ ___/z/___
2. wish ___es___ ___/əz/___
3. aunt ___s___ ___/s/___
4. flower _____ _____
5. park _____ _____

6. touch _____ _____
7. month _____ _____
8. tree _____ _____
9. dress _____ _____
10. valley _____ _____

11. industry _____ _____
12. swallow _____ _____
13. cliff _____ _____
14. bath _____ _____
15. bathe _____ _____

► **Practice 4. Basic subject-verb agreement.** (Chart 6-2)
Circle the correct verb.

1. The weather (*is / are*) cold.
2. Vegetables (*is / are*) good for you.
3. Each boy (*has / have*) his own locker in the gym.
4. A dog (*barks / bark*).
5. Dogs (*barks / bark*).
6. Ann (*is / are*) at home.
7. Ann and Sue (*is / are*) at home.
8. Every boy and girl (*is / are*) here.
9. A boy and a girl (*is / are*) in the street.
10. Eating vegetables (*is / are*) good for you.

▶ **Practice 5. Subject-verb agreement: using expressions of quantity.** (Chart 6-3)
Complete the sentences with *is* or *are*.

1. Some of Highway 21 _____ closed due to flooding.

2. Some of the highways _____ closed due to flooding.

3. A lot of that movie _____ full of violence.

4. A lot of movies _____ full of violence.

5. Half of the pizza _____ for you and half _____ for me.

6. Half of the pizzas _____ vegetarian.

7. Most of my friends _____ people I met in school.

8. Every one of my friends _____ a sports fan.

9. The number of desks in that classroom _____ thirty-five.

10. A number of stores _____ closed today because of the holiday.

▶ **Practice 6. Subject-verb agreement: using expressions of quantity.** (Chart 6-3)
Circle the correct verb.

1. A large part of our town (*have* / *has*) been badly damaged by a big fire.

2. Most of the houses (*was* / *were*) destroyed by the fire.

3. Most of the house (*was* / *were*) destroyed by the fire.

4. One of the houses (*was* / *were*) destroyed by the fire.

5. Each of the houses (*is* / *are*) in ruins.

6. Each house (*is* / *are*) in ruins.

7. Every one of the houses (*has* / *have*) serious damage.

8. Every house (*has* / *have*) serious damage.

9. None of the houses (*has* / *have*) escaped damage.

▶ **Practice 7. Subject-verb agreement: using *there* + *be*.** (Chart 6-4)
Circle the correct verb.

1. There (*is* / *are*) a cup on the table.

2. There (*is* / *are*) some cups on the table.

3. There (*is* / *are*) a lot of people in the line for the movie.

4. There (*is* / *are*) a snack bar in the lobby of the theater.

5. There (*wasn't* / *weren't*) any hurricanes in Florida last year.

6. There (*was* / *were*) a terrible tsunami in Asia in 2004.

7. Why (*isn't* / *aren't*) there any windows in the classroom?

8. Why (*isn't* / *aren't*) there a teacher in the classroom?

9. There (*has* / *have*) been an ongoing problem with the color printer.

10. There (*has* / *have*) been a lot of problems with the color printer.

► **Practice 8. Subject-verb agreement: some irregularities.** (Chart 6-5)
Circle the correct verb.

1. States (*is* / *are*) political units.

2. The United States (*is* / *are*) in North America.

3. The news in that newspaper (*is* / *are*) biased.

4. Economics (*is* / *are*) an important area of study.

5. Diabetes (*is* / *are*) an illness. Mumps (*is* / *are*) another kind of illness. Rabies (*is* / *are*) a disease you can get from being bitten by an infected animal.

6. One hundred meters (*isn't* / *aren't*) a long distance to travel by car.

7. Five minutes (*isn't* / *aren't*) too long to wait.

8. Six and four (*is* / *are*) ten.

9. People (*is* / *are*) interesting.

10. English (*is* / *are*) a common language.

11. The English (*is* / *are*) friendly people.

12. The elderly in my country (*is* / *are*) given free medical care.

13. Four colorful fish (*is* / *are*) swimming in the fish tank.

14. The police (*is* / *are*) coming to investigate the accident.

► **Practice 9. Subject-verb agreement.** (Charts 6-2 → 6-5)
Complete the sentences with the present tense of the appropriate verb from the list. Some verbs may be used more than once.

be	contain	cost	drive	like	make	remind

1. There _____ an old barn near our town. The barn has been converted to a bookstore, and its name is The Old Barn Bookstore.

2. It's a very popular place, especially on weekends. People _____ it a lot. They _____ out to the barn on weekends.

3. It's about twenty miles from downtown. Twenty miles _____ a long drive, but the bookstore is worth the drive.

4. A lot of the books in The Old Barn Bookstore _____ not new books. There _____ a lot of used books, old books, and even valuable antique books.

5. There _____ a large number of beautiful art books too. Each one _____ excellent photographs of famous pieces of art. Most of these books _____ quite expensive.

6. I'm thinking about buying a few nice art books there. One of the books _____ over a hundred dollars because it is very valuable. It has an autograph and an inscription by Ernest Hemingway.

7. There _____ a small café in The Old Barn Bookstore too. You can sit there for hours if you want, browsing through the books you are thinking of buying. The number of food items on the menu _____ very small, but about twenty different kinds of coffee _____ served.

8. Last Sunday I was browsing through some books when suddenly I heard several people speaking French. When I looked up, I saw six people at the next table, all speaking excitedly. I used to understand French, but now French _____ very difficult for me to understand. However, hearing French always _____ me of my days as a student and _____ me feel young again.

▶ **Practice 10. Subject-verb agreement.** (Charts 6-2 → 6-5)
Circle the correct verb.

1. Each skater in the competition (*has / have*) trained since childhood.

2. A convention of English teachers from all over the world (*take / takes*) place every spring.

3. Some of the new movies (*is / are*) good, but a lot of them (*have / has*) too much violence.

4. We saw a film about India last night. Some of the movie (*was /were*) fascinating, and there (*was / were*) a lot of beautiful mountain scenes.

5. Three-fourths of the patients who (*take / takes*) this new medicine report improvement.

6. Almost three-quarters of the surface of the earth (*is / are*) covered by water.

7. There (*is / are*) 100 senators in the United States Senate. The number of votes necessary for a simple majority (*is / are*) 51.

8. There (*has / have*) been some encouraging news about pandas in recent years. There (*is / are*) more pandas living today than there (*was / were*) ten years ago.

9. The United Arab Emirates (*is / are*) a country in the Middle East.

10. The *New York Times* (*is / are*) an important newspaper.

11. Economics (*is / are*) impossible for me to understand.

12. Diabetes (*is /are*) an illness. People who (*has / have*) it must be careful with their diet.

13. Five dollars (*is / are*) too much to pay for a pencil!

14. The English (*speak / speaks*) with an accent that is different from the American accent.

15. The handicapped (*use / uses*) a special entrance in this building.

► **Practice 11. Subject-verb agreement.** (Chapters 1–6)
Complete the sentences with the correct form of the given verb. Use any appropriate tense.

1. Nearly 90 percent of the people in our town always (*vote*) _____ in local elections.

2. In recent years, a number of students (*participate*) _____ in language programs abroad.

3. The number of students who knew the answer to the last question on the exam (*be*) _____ very low.

4. Every one of the boys and girls in the school (*know*) _____ what to do if the fire alarm rings.

5. A lot of people in the United States (*speak*) _____ and (*understand*) _____ _____ Spanish.

6. Why (*be*) _____ the police standing over there right now?

7. Why (*broadcast*) _____ most of the television stations _____ news at the same hour every night?

8. Some of the most important books for my report (*be*) _____ not available in the school library, so I'll have to look for information on the internet.

9. Recently there (*be*) _____ times when I have seriously considered dropping out of school.

10. Not one of the women in my office (*receive*) _____ a promotion in the past two years. All of the promotions (*go*) _____ to men.

11. The news on the radio and TV stations (*confirm*) _____ that a serious storm is approaching our city.

12. Geography (*be*) _____ fascinating. Mathematics (*be*) _____ fascinating. I love those subjects!

13. Mathematics and geography (*be*) _____ my favorite subjects.

14. By law, every man, woman, and child (*have*) _____ the right to free speech. It is guaranteed in our constitution.

15. (*Be, not*) _____ sugar and pineapple the leading crops in Hawaii now?

16. Why (*be*) _____ there a shortage of certified school teachers at the present time?

17. How many states in the United States (*begin*) _____ with the letter "A"?*

18. The United States (*consist*) _____ of 50 states.

19. What places in the world (*have*) _____ no snakes?

20. Politics (*be*) _____ a constant source of interest to me.

21. (*Be*) _____ there ever any doubt in your mind about the outcome of the election? You were sure that Garcia was going to win, weren't you?

---

*See the Answer Key for the answer to this question.

Chapter 7
Nouns

▶ **Practice 1. Regular and irregular plural nouns.** (Chart 7-1)
Write the plural forms of the given nouns.

1. one car, two _____
2. one woman, two _____
3. one match, two _____
4. one mouse, two _____
5. one city, two _____
6. one donkey, two _____
7. one half, two _____
8. one chief, two _____

9. one class, two _____
10. one foot, two _____
11. one hero, two _____
12. one piano, two _____
13. one video, two _____
14. one basis, two _____
15. one bacterium, two _____
16. one series, two _____

▶ **Practice 2. Regular and irregular plural nouns.** (Chart 7-1)
Complete the sentences with the correct plural form of the nouns in the list. Use each word once.

belief	fish	monkey	radio	thief
child	kilo	potato	species	tooth

1. I had my favorite vegetable for dinner: delicious fried _____.
2. At the zoo, we saw a lot of _____ jumping around in the trees.
3. The police caught the two _____ who had stolen over 100
   _____ from people's cars.
4. The shopping mall has a playground for _____.
5. Our baby got two new _____ this week!
6. The two families found that they hold the same _____; they believe in the same
   things.
7. Some people think that whales are a species of _____, but they are not; they are
   mammals.
8. The adult male of some _____ of bears weighs about 600 _____.

► **Practice 3. Final -s / -es.** (Chapter 6 and Chart 7-1)
Add final **-s** / **-es** where necessary. Do not change, add, or omit any other words in the sentences.

1. A bird care_∧ˢ for its feather_∧ˢ by cleaning them with its beak.

2. There are many occupation in the world. Doctor take care of sick people. Pilot fly airplane. Farmer raise crop. Shepherd take care of sheep.

3. An architect design building. An archeologist dig in the ground to find object from past civilizations.

4. The first modern computer were developed in the 1930s and 1940s. Computer were not commercially available until the 1950s.

5. There are several factory in my hometown. The glass factory employ many people.

6. Kangaroo are Australian animal. They are not found on any of the other continent, except in zoo.

7. Mosquito are found everywhere in the world, including the Arctic.

8. At one time, many people believed that tomato were poisonous.

► **Practice 4. Possessive nouns.** (Chart 7-2)
Answer the questions for each sentence.

1. My parents' house is over 100 years old.
   a. What is the possessive noun? _____
   b. How many parents are there, one or two? _____
   c. What two nouns does the possessive (s') connect? _____ + _____

2. Safety is a parent's concern.
   a. What is the possessive noun? _____
   b. How many parents are there, one or more than one? _____
   c. What two nouns does the possessive ('s) connect? _____ + _____

3. Cats' eyes shine in the dark.
   a. What is the possessive noun? _____
   b. How many cats are there, one or many? _____
   c. What two nouns does the possessive (s') connect? _____ + _____

4. My cat's eyes are big and green.
   a. What is the possessive noun? _____
   b. How many cats are there, one or several? _____
   c. What two nouns does the possessive ('s) connect? _____ + _____

5. Do you know Mary's brother?

    a. What is the possessive noun? _____

    b. What belongs to Mary? _____

    c. What two nouns does the possessive ('s) connect? _____ + _____

6. Do you know Mary's brothers?

    a. What is the possessive noun? _____

    b. What belongs to Mary? _____

    c. What two nouns does the possessive ('s) connect? _____ + _____

7. My brothers' team won the game.

    a. What is the possessive noun? _____

    b. How many brothers do I have, one or more than one? _____

    c. What two nouns does the possessive (s') connect? _____ + _____

8. My brother's team won the game.

    a. What is the possessive noun? _____

    b. How many brothers do I have, one or more than one? _____

    c. What two nouns does the possessive ('s) connect? _____ + _____

▶ **Practice 5. Possessive nouns.** (Chart 7-2)
Check the correct number for the words in **bold**.

1. The **teacher's** office is down the hall.   ☐ one   ☐ more than one

2. The **teachers'** office is down the hall.   ☐ one   ☐ more than one

3. My **sisters'** clothes are all over my bed.   ☐ one   ☐ more than one

4. I visited the **boy's** house.   ☐ one   ☐ more than one

5. I agree with the **judges'** decision.   ☐ one   ☐ more than one

6. The customer service representative must
listen to the **customers'** complaints.   ☐ one   ☐ more than one

7. The professor discussed the **student's** assignment.   ☐ one   ☐ more than one

8. The flight attendant put the **passenger's** bags
in the overhead compartment.   ☐ one   ☐ more than one

▶ **Practice 6. Possessive nouns.** (Chart 7-2)
Make the *italicized* nouns possessive by adding apostrophes and final *-s* / *-es*. Cross out and change a letter if necessary.

1. He put the mail in his *secretary* _'s___ mailbox.

2. There are three secretaries in our office. The *secretar~~y~~ ies'___* mailboxes are in the hallway.

3. Tom has two cats. The *cat* _____ food and water dishes are on a shelf in the laundry room.

4. I have one cat. My *cat* _____ feet are white, but the rest of her is black.

5. My *supervisor* _____ names are Ms. Anderson and Mr. Gomez.

6. Your *supervisor* _____ name is Ms. Wright.

7. My twin *baby* _____ eyes are dark blue, just like their father's eyes.

8. My *baby* _____ eyes are dark blue, just like her father's eyes.

9. Olga's *child* _____ name is Olaf.

10. José and Alicia's *children* _____ names are Pablo and Gabriela.

11. I'm interested in other *people* _____ ideas.

12. All of the performers in the play did well. The audience applauded the *actor* _____ excellent performances.

13. An *actor* _____ income is uncertain.

▶ **Practice 7. Possessive nouns.** (Chart 7-2)
Circle the correct word or phrase.

1. My (*mother's* / *mothers'*) name is Maria.

2. Both my (*grandmother's* / *grandmothers'*) names were Maria too.

3. The (*teacher's* / *teachers'*) class is so big that the students in the back of the room can't hear her when she talks.

4. My (*bosses'* / *boss'*) name is Carl.

5. An (*employee's* / *employees'*) wallet was found under a table at the (*employee's* / *employees'*) cafeteria yesterday.

6. Here's the directory for the department store: the (*mens'* / *men's*) department is on the first floor; the (*women's* / *womens'*) department is on the second floor; the (*children's* / *childrens'*) department is on the third floor. On the third floor, the (*girl's* / *girls'*) clothes are on the right side, and the (*boy's* / *boys'*) clothes are on the left side.

▶ **Practice 8. Nouns as adjectives.** (Chart 7-3)
Underline the adjective. Check the sentences where a noun is used as an adjective.

1. ____ It's an *expensive ticket*.
2. ____ It's a *theater ticket*.
3. ____ It's a *small theater*.
4. ____ It's a *movie theater*.
5. ____ It's a *family movie*.

6. ____ They are *family movies*.
7. ____ It's a *computer desk*.
8. ____ It's a *hair dryer*.
9. ____ They are *window washers*.
10. ____ It's a *gas station*.

▶ **Practice 9. Nouns as adjectives.** (Chart 7-3)
Complete the sentences with the given nouns. Use the singular or plural form as appropriate.

1. They sell ____groceries____ at that store. It is a ____grocery____ store. (*grocery*)

2. They raise ____chickens____ on their farm. It's a ____chicken____ farm. (*chicken*)

3. I like _____ salads. I like salads that contain _____. (*tomato*)

4. A friend gave us a wooden frame for _____. It's a very attractive wooden _____ frame. (*picture*)

5. I have a _____ garden. I grow several different kinds of _____. (*flower*)

6. Some people are addicted to _____. They are _____ addicts. (*drug*)

7. This carton holds one dozen _____. It's an _____ carton. (*egg*)

8. We drove down an old, narrow highway that had only _____. We drove down a _____ highway. (*two + lane*)

9. I gave a _____ speech in class. My speech lasted for _____. (*five + minute*)

10. The Watkins family lives in a _____ house. Any house that is _____ usually needs a lot of repairs. (*sixty + year + old*)

11. You need a special license to drive a _____. Ed has been a _____ driver for twenty-five years. (*truck*)

12. Susan programs _____. There are good jobs for _____ programmers everywhere. (*computer*)

▶ **Practice 10. Nouns as adjectives.** (Chart 7-3)
Choose the correct completion.

1. A table in a kitchen is a _____.
   a. kitchen table   b. table kitchen   c. kitchen's table

2. The two tables in my bedroom are my _____.
   a. bedrooms tables   b. tables bedroom   c. bedroom tables

3. I have an office at home. It is my _____.
   a. office home   b. home office   c. office of home

4. A lot of people have offices in their homes. They have _____.
   a. home offices   b. homes offices   c. homes office

5. There are two phone lines in my house, one for my home and one for my office. One is my home phone and the other is my _____.
   a. phone office   b. office phone   c. offices phone

6. There is a sink in the kitchen and one in each bathroom. We have two bathrooms. So we have one kitchen sink and two _____.
   a. bathrooms sinks   b. bathroom sink   c. bathroom sinks

7. In the back of our house, we grow vegetables in a garden. It's a _____.
   a. vegetable garden   b. vegetables garden   c. garden vegetables

8. We have two trees that grow cherries. They are _____.
   a. tree cherries   b. cherry trees   c. cherries trees

▶ **Practice 11. Nouns as adjectives.** (Chart 7-3)
Complete the sentences. Write the correct phrase using the two nouns in *italics*.

1. That *handbook* is for *students*. It is a ___student handbook___.

2. There was a *party* to celebrate Lynn's *birthday*. There was a _____ for Lynn.

3. The retirees receive *checks* from the *government* every month. They receive a

_____ every month.

4. The *seats* in the *airplane* are very small. The _____ are very

small.

5. The *pajamas* are made of *cotton*. They are _____ .

6. There were no *rooms* in the local *hotels* that were available. There were no available

_____ .

7. Their *baby* is *ten months old*. They have a _____ .

8. Our *trip* lasted for *three days*. We took a _____ .

9. Their *apartment* has *three rooms*. It is a _____ .

10. The professor asked us to write a *paper* of *five pages*. She asked us to write a

_____ .

11. Luigi is a *singer*. He sings in *operas*. He's a famous _____ .

12. A convention for people who collect *stamps* is being held at City Center. My uncle is a *collector*.

He has been a _____ since he was a boy.

▶ **Practice 12. Count and noncount nouns.** (Chart 7-4)
Look at the *italicized* nouns. Write "C" above the count nouns and "NC" above the noncount
nouns.

                 NC   C NC NC NC   C

1. We bought a lot of *food*. We bought some *eggs, bread, milk, coffee,* and *bananas.*

2. I get a lot of *mail*. I get some *letters, magazines, catalogs,* and *bills* almost every day.

3. *Euros, pounds,* and *dollars* are different kinds of *money.*

4. Alma doesn't wear much *jewelry*. She wears a *ring* and sometimes *earrings.*

5. A *language* consists of *vocabulary* and *grammar.*

6. We need some *furniture* for the patio: a *table*, six *chairs*, and an *umbrella.*

▶ **Practice 13. Count and noncount nouns.** (Charts 7-4 → 7-6)
Circle the correct completion.

1. Every day I learn some more new (*word / words*) in English.

2. Olga knows (*an / some*) American slang.

3. There are a lot of (*car / cars*) on the highway at rush hour.

4. We got here so fast! There wasn't (*much / many*) traffic on the highway.

5. We ate a tuna (*sandwich / sandwiches*) for lunch.

6. We got only (*some / one*) good picture on our trip.

7. That website contains (*an / some*) excellent information.

8. That is (*a very / very*) good news!

▶ **Practice 14. Count and noncount nouns.** (Charts 7-4 → 7-6)
Add final **-s** / **-es** to the nouns in *italics* if necessary. Do not add, omit, or change any other words. Some sentences have no errors.

1. Jackie has brown *hair* and gray *eye*$_\wedge$.

2. My parents gave me some good *advice*.

3. I always drink *water* when I'm hot and thirsty.

4. Do winning athletes need *luck*?

5. Our country has made a lot of *progress* in the last 25 years.

6. How many *class* are you taking this semester?

7. Yesterday we received some *fax* from our lawyer.

▶ **Practice 15. Count and noncount nouns.** (Charts 7-4 → 7-6)
Circle the correct word or phrase.

1. It takes (*courage* / *a courage*) to be an astronaut.

2. We bought (*some* / *a*) new clothing.

3. The baby needs a new pair of (*shoe* / *shoes*).

4. The garbage truck comes on Monday, Wednesday, and Friday mornings to pick up the (*garbage* / *garbages*).

5. I ordered twelve (*glass* / *glasses*) from a site on the internet. When they arrived, one (*glass* / *glasses*) was broken.

6. Many people need to wear (*glass* / *glasses*) to see better. The lenses should be made of (*glass* / *glasses*) that doesn't break easily.

7. I filled out a report for (*a lost luggage* / *some lost luggage*) at the airport, but I'm not optimistic. I wonder if they find (*much* / *many*) lost suitcases.

8. Would you like to go out tonight? I don't have (*much* / *many*) homework, and I'd like to go out and have (*some* / *a*) fun.

9. Ireland is famous for its beautiful green (*hill* / *hills*). Ireland has (*a lovely* / *lovely*) scenery, but it often has (*a damp* / *damp*) weather.

10. The four-leaf clover is a symbol of (*a good* / *good*) luck in Ireland.

► **Practice 16. Basic article usage.** (Chart 7-7)
Complete the sentences with *a*, *an*, or *Ø*. Capitalize as necessary.

1. _A_ car has wheels.
2. _An_ airplane has wings.
3. _Ø_ Energy is necessary to move cars and airplanes.
4. ____ banana has a long, narrow shape.
5. ____ apple is round.
6. ____ fruit is nutritious.
7. ____ sodium is a mineral.

8. ____ air is a gas.
9. ____ rice is a kind of grass.
10. ____ elephant lives a long time.
11. ____ zebra has black and white stripes.
12. ____ football is an international sport.
13. ____ football is oval in the United States and round in the rest of the world.
14. ____ football player has to be strong.

► **Practice 17. Basic article usage.** (Chart 7-7)
Complete the sentences with *a*, *an*, or *some*.

1. I asked _____a_____ question.
2. The students asked _____some_____ questions.
3. I got _____an_____ answer.
4. I received _____ information.
5. Chess is _____ game.
6. The children played _____ games at the party.
7. I heard _____ news about the hurricane.
8. I read _____ newspaper.
9. My professor wrote _____ letter to the newspaper.
10. I wrote _____ email to my professor.
11. I got _____ mail from the university.
12. Susan left _____ things in her car.
13. Matt bought _____ printer.
14. The printer needs _____ ink.

► **Practice 18. General article usage.** (Chart 7-8)
Read each conversation. Circle the letter of the sentence that explains what the speakers are talking about.

1. A: Where's the teacher? I have a question.
    B: I'm not sure.

    a. Speaker A is asking about any teacher.
    b. Speaker A is asking about a teacher Speaker B is familiar with.

2. A: I put down the phone and now I can't find it.
    B: I do that a lot!

    a. Speaker A is referring to a phone Speaker B is familiar with.
    b. Speaker A is referring to any phone.

3. A: Could you pick up some eggs and rice at the store? We'll have the rice for dinner.

   B: Sure.

       a. In the first sentence, *rice* is general. In the second sentence, *rice* is specific.

       b. In both sentences, *rice* is specific.

4. A: Bananas have a lot of potassium.

   B: They're very healthy.

       a. Speaker A is referring to a specific group of bananas.

       b. Speaker A is referring to bananas in general.

5. A: Does Saturn have a moon that orbits it?

   B: I don't know!

       a. Speaker A is talking about a specific moon.

       b. Speaker A is talking about any moon.

6. A: Have you seen the moon tonight?

   B: Yes! It's spectacular.

       a. The speakers are referring to the moon that goes around the Earth.

       b. The speakers are referring to any moon in the solar system.

▶ **Practice 19. General article usage.** (Chart 7-8)
Correct the errors.

1. It's beautiful today. Sun is shining and sky is clear.

2. There's a boy on a swing, and a girl is pushing him. Boy is about five years old, and girl is about eight years old.

3. The penguins live in Antarctica. The polar bears don't live in Antarctica.

4. Which is more important — the love or the money?

5. A: What does this word mean?

   B: Do you have dictionary? Look up word in dictionary.

6. A: Watch out! There's a bee buzzing around!

   B: Where? I don't see it. Ouch! It stung me! I didn't see bee, but I felt it!

▶ **Practice 20. Using articles.** (Charts 7-7 and 7-8)
Complete the sentences with *a* / *an* or *the*.

1. A: Let's take _____ break. Do you want to go to _____ movie?

   B: That's _____ good idea. Which movie do you want to see?

   A: _____ movie at the Rialto Theater is a comedy. Let's see that one.

2. A: So, students, who knows _____ answer to this question?

   B: I do!

3. A: Professor Li, I have _____ question about the assignment.

    B: What's your question?

4. A: There's _____ spot on my shirt!

    B: Here. Take out _____ spot with this spot remover.

5. A: Listen! I hear _____ noise! Do you hear it?

    B: Yes, I hear something.

6. A: What was _____ noise that you heard?

    B: I think it was _____ mouse.

    A: But we don't have any mice in _____ house!

    B: Well, maybe it was just _____ wind.

▶ **Practice 21. Using articles.** (Charts 7-7 and 7-8)
Complete the sentences with *a / an, the,* or **Ø**. Capitalize as necessary.

1. ___Ø___ Lightning is ___a___ flash of light. It is usually followed by ___Ø___ thunder.

2. Last night we had ___a___ terrible storm. Our children were frightened by ___the___ thunder.

3. _____ circles are _____ round geometric figures.

4. _____ circle with _____ slash drawn through it is an international symbol meaning "Do not do this!" For example, _____ circle in _____ illustration means "No Smoking."

5. _____ inventor of _____ modern cell phone was Dr. Martin Cooper. He made the first call on the first portable handset in 1973 when he was _____ employee of the Motorola company.

6. Frank Lloyd Wright is _____ name of _____ famous architect. He is _____ architect who designed the Guggenheim Museum in New York. He also designed _____ hotel in Tokyo. _____ hotel was designed to withstand _____ earthquakes.

7. There was _____ small earthquake in California last year. _____ earthquake caused _____ damage to several buildings, but fortunately, no one was killed.

▶ **Practice 22. Expressions of quantity with count and noncount nouns.** (Chart 7-9)

Draw a line through the expressions that <u>cannot</u> be used to complete the sentences. Item 1 has been started for you.

1. Linda did _____ work last Saturday.
   a. ~~three~~
   b. ~~several~~
   c. some
   d. a lot of
   e. too much
   f. too many
   g. a few
   h. a little
   i. a number of
   j. a great deal of
   k. hardly any
   l. no

2. Henry is planning _____ projects for next month.
   a. three
   b. several
   c. some
   d. a lot of
   e. too much
   f. too many
   g. a few
   h. a little
   i. a number of
   j. a great deal of
   k. hardly any
   l. no

▶ **Practice 23. Expressions of quantity with count and noncount nouns.** (Chart 7-9)

Complete the sentences with *much* or *many*. Also write the plural forms of the nouns as necessary. In some sentences, you will need to circle the correct verb in parentheses.

1. How _____*many*_____ ~~computer~~ *computers* are there in the language lab?

2. How _____*much*_____ equipment is there in the language lab?

3. How _____*many*_____ ~~child~~ *children* (is / (are)) in Ms. Thompson's class?

4. How _____ tooth do babies usually have when they're born?

5. Ellen and Rick have traveled widely. They've visited _____ country.

6. I don't know _____ American slang.

7. Enrique hasn't made _____ progress in learning to play the piano. That's because he doesn't spend _____ time practicing.

8. How _____ DVDs do you usually rent during a month?

9. My hair is all frizzy today. There (*is* / *are*) too _____ humidity in the air.

10. I haven't done _____ reading lately.

11. There (*was* / *were*) so _____ smog in Los Angeles yesterday that you couldn't see any of the hills or mountains from the city.

12. I didn't know _____ grammar before taking this course.

13. How _____ active volcano (*is / are*) there in the world today?

14. Politicians give _____ speech during their careers.

▶ **Practice 24. Expressions of quantity with count and noncount nouns.**
(Chart 7-9)

Circle the letter of all the possible completions.

1. Pat bought a few _____ at the art show.
   a. pictures
   b. photographs
   c. art
   d. ceramic bowls

2. Mike bought some _____ at the supermarket.
   a. milk
   b. orange
   c. magazines
   d. flashlight battery

3. There were several _____ on the plane.
   a. child
   b. people
   c. babies
   d. passenger

4. There was a little _____ on the table.
   a. food
   b. cream
   c. coffee
   d. sandwiches

5. We have plenty of _____ for everyone.
   a. food
   b. pizza
   c. drinks
   d. hot dog

6. Can you bring a couple of _____ with you when you come to the party?
   a. ice
   b. hamburger
   c. bottles of soda
   d. water

7. I don't have many _____ about this.
   a. thoughts
   b. knowledge
   c. ideas
   d. information

8. Do Charlie and Kate have much _____?
   a. problems
   b. children
   c. fun
   d. work

9. I know a number of _____.
   a. people
   b. things
   c. professors
   d. news

10. They don't have a great deal of _____.
    a. intelligence
    b. information
    c. facts
    d. education

▶ **Practice 25. Using *a few* and *few*; *a little* and *little*.** (Chart 7-10)
In each pair of sentences, check the sentence that has the *larger number or quantity* of something.

1. a. We have a little money. ✓
   b. We have little money. ___

2. a. They know few people. ___
   b. They know a few people. ___

3. a. She has very little patience. ___
   b. She has a little patience. ___

4. a. I speak some Spanish. ___
   b. I speak little Spanish. ___

5. a. Marta asked few questions. ___
   b. Marta asked a few questions. ___

▶ **Practice 26. Using *a few* and *few*; *a little* and *little*.** (Chart 7-10)
Complete the sentences. Write the letter of the correct completion.

1. Belinda learned to skate very quickly. At first, she fell down ____ times, but now she very rarely falls down.
   a. few   b. a few   c. a little

2. The police didn't have a good description of the bank robber. ____ witnesses actually saw his face.
   a. few   b. a few   c. little

3. Please pass the cream. I like ____ cream in my coffee. It tastes better.
   a. a few   b. a little   c. very few

4. You'd better know the answers when Professor Simpson calls on you in class tomorrow. He has ____ patience with students who are not prepared.
   a. very little   b. very few   c. a little

5. Before the hurricane, the stores were crowded with people buying supplies. By the time I got to a store, ____ flashlight batteries were left, and ____ bottled water was available.
   a. very few / very little   b. very little / very little   c. very little / very few

6. Come over to our house tonight. Peter is bringing his guitar. He'll play ____ folk music, and we'll sing ____ old songs.
   a. few / little   b. a few / a little   c. a little / a few

7. To make this sauce, first cook ____ onions in ____ oil.
   a. few / little   b. a few / a little   c. little / few

▶ **Practice 27. Using *a few* and *few*; *a little* and *little*.** (Chart 7-10)
Without changing the meaning of the sentences, replace the *italicized* words with ***a few, few, a little***, or ***little***.

       a little
1. If you put ~~some~~ sugar on those berries, they will taste sweeter.

                                                                    a few
2. Many people live to be more than 100 years old, but only ~~some~~ people live to be 110 years old.

3. Many cities in the world have a population of over a million, and *some* cities have a population of more than ten million.

4. You might reach your goal if you put forth *some* more effort.

5. The professor lectured very clearly. At the end of the class, *not many* students had questions.

6. I have to go to the post office because I have *some* letters to mail.

7. Every day Max goes to his mailbox, but it is usually empty. He gets *almost no* mail.

8. My friend arrived in the United States *some* months ago.

9. I think you could use *some* help. Let me give you *some* advice.

10. Margaret likes sweet tea. She usually adds *some* honey to her tea. Sometimes she adds *some* milk too.

▶ **Practice 28. Singular expressions of quantity: *one, each, every.*** (Chart 7-11)
Choose the correct word from the list. Write the correct singular or plural form. Some words may be used more than once.

child	goose	neighbor	✓ state
chimpanzee	man	puppy	woman

1. There is only one _____*state*_____ in the United States that is completely surrounded by water: Hawaii.

2. One of the _____*states*_____ in the United States that shares a border with Canada is Vermont.

3. Our dog had six puppies. I wanted to keep them all, but I couldn't. I kept one of the _____, but I gave away the other five.

4. There were six puppies. One _____ was black and white, and five were all black.

5. The children enjoyed the zoo. One of the _____ wandered away from the group, but she was quickly found at the snack bar.

6. The children particularly liked watching the chimpanzees. One _____, a boy named Kevin, seemed to be having a conversation with one of the _____.

7. One of our _____ gave a welcoming party for a new family who had just moved to our neighborhood from Ecuador.

8. There were several men riding on motorcycles together. One _____ seemed to be their leader. He was riding in front of the group.

9. The geese are flying in a V-formation. One _____ is at the point of the V, apparently leading the whole flock.

10. Our book club consists of fifteen women who have been together in the club for more than twenty years. One of the _____ was just elected mayor of our town.

► **Practice 29. *One, each, every.*** (Chart 7-11)
Correct the errors in the *italicized* words. Not every sentence has an error.

1. According to the Constitution of the United States, *every persons* has certain rights.

2. One of *rights* is the right to vote.

3. Each of *states* is represented by two senators in the U.S. Senate.

4. *Each of* senator is elected for a six-year term.

5. The number of representatives in the House of Representatives depends on the population of
   each state.

6. For example, Nevada, one of *the very small state*, has only three representatives, but New York, a
   populous state, has 29 representatives.

7. Every one of *citizen* is eligible to vote for president, but not every *citizen* exercises this right.

8. In some countries, voting is compulsory. Every *citizens* must vote.

► **Practice 30. Using *of* in expressions of quantity.** (Chart 7-12)
Complete the sentences with *of* or **Ø**.

1. Several _____ my colleagues are going to the lecture at the library tonight.

2. I have several _____ colleagues who have PhDs.

3. Many _____ the houses in New Orleans were lost to the floods that occurred after Hurricane
   Katrina.

4. These days, _____ new houses are being built with stronger materials to withstand
   hurricanes.

5. A few _____ children are born with exceptional musical talent.

6. Some _____ the children in Mr. McFarlane's music class are playing in a recital.

7. Most _____ people like to hear compliments.

8. My cousin won a million _____ dollars on a game show.

9. Many _____ places in the world use wind as a source of energy. Some _____ these places
   supply energy to thousands _____ homes and businesses.

10. There was hardly any _____ rain this spring. As a result, hardly any _____ my flowers
    bloomed.

11. To form the plural of most _____ the words in English, we add an *-s* or *-es* at the end. Not
    every word forms its plural in this way, however. Some _____ words have irregular endings.

Complete the crossword puzzle. Use the clues under the puzzle and the words in the list. All the words in the puzzle are from the charts in Chapter 7. All the sentences are well-known sayings in English.

all	every	many	mice	some
an	man	men	one	two

Across

3. _____ good things must come to an end.

4. You can't make an omelet without breaking _____ eggs.

6. A _____ is known by his friends.

8. _____ cloud has a silver lining.

Down

1. _____ heads are better than one.

2. _____ picture is worth a thousand words.

3. _____ apple a day keeps the doctor away.

5. When the cat's away, the _____ will play.

6. Too _____ cooks spoil the broth.

7. Dead _____ tell no tales.

Chapter 8
Pronouns

▶ **Practice 1. Personal pronouns.** (Chart 8-1)
Draw a circle around each pronoun that has an antecedent. Draw an arrow from the pronoun to its antecedent.

1. Bob works for Trans-Ocean Airlines. (He) flies cargo across the Pacific Ocean.

2. Mr. and Mrs. Nobriega are moving. They have bought a house in the suburbs.

3. There goes my English teacher. Do you know her?

4. The baby just began to walk. She is eleven months old.

5. A new kind of car is being advertised. It runs on a battery.

6. There are two hawks up there on the telephone wire. Do you see them?

7. Sorry, Mr. Frank is not in the office now. Please call him at home.

8. We have a dog and a cat. They are part of our family.

▶ **Practice 2. Personal pronouns.** (Chart 8-1)
Circle the words in *italics* that are grammatically correct.

1. Sarah and (*I / me*) are taking a yoga class.

2. I'm going to tell you something, but don't tell anyone. It's just between you and (*I / me*).

3. Carlos and Julia were at the movies together. I saw (*they / them*). (*They / Them*) were holding hands.

4. Where are my papers? I left (*it / them*) right here on the table.

5. I have (*my / mine*) problems, and you have (*your / yours*).

6. Jim and Helena both work from home. He works at (*he / his*) computer all day, and she works at (*her / hers*). At five o'clock sharp they both stop (*they / their*) work.

7. My aunt is only five years older than I am. (*She and I / Her and me*) are very close. We are like sisters. (*Our / Ours*) friends and relatives treat (*our / us*) like sisters.

8. I studied Latin when I was in high school. Of course, nobody speaks Latin today, but Latin was very useful to (*me / I*). Because I understand (*it / its*) grammar, I can understand grammar in other languages. And my vocabulary is bigger because of (*it / its*) too.

9. When baby giraffes are born, (*they / its*) are six feet tall, taller than the average person. (*They / It*) sometimes grow an inch a day, and they double (*its / their*) height in one year.

10. Did you know Mauna Kea in Hawaii is actually the tallest mountain in the world? If you measure it from (*its* / *it's*) base at the bottom of the Pacific Ocean to (*its* / *it's*) peak, it has a height of 33,476 feet (10,203 meters). (*Its* / *It's*) taller than Mount Everest.

▶ **Practice 3. Personal pronouns: agreement with generic nouns and indefinite pronouns.** (Chart 8-2)

Circle the letter of the correct completions. In some sentences, both choices are correct.

1. All students must bring ____ books to class every day.
   a. his   b. their

2. Each girl in the class must bring ____ books to class every day.
   a. her   b. his or her

3. Everyone on the tennis team must leave ____ cell phone number with the coach.
   a. his or her   b. their

4. Everybody on the men's bowling team brings ____ own bowling ball to the bowling alley.
   a. his   b. his or her

5. Everyone should know how to do ____ job.
   a. his or her   b. their

6. Girls, whose keys are these? Somebody left ____ keys on the table.
   a. their   b. her

7. Nobody in the Boy Scout troop failed ____ tests. Everybody passed.
   a. his   b. their

▶ **Practice 4. Personal pronouns: agreement with collective nouns.**
(Charts 8-2 and 8-3)

Complete the sentences with a word or phrase from the list. You may use an item more than once.

her	his or her	its	them
his	it	their	they

1. Tonight's audience is special. Everyone in _____ is a member of the fire department or the police department. The show is being performed especially for _____.

2. When the play was over, the audience arose from _____ seats and applauded wildly.

3. The actors bowed to the audience's applause. The leading man took _____ bow first, and then the leading lady took _____ bow.

4. The faculty of the philosophy department is very small. In fact, _____ has only two professors. _____ share an office.

5. Well, Mia, I'm sorry you're having problems. Everyone has _____ problems, goodness knows!

6. A notice sent home with each girl on the girls' volleyball team said: "The girls' volleyball team is playing at Cliffside on Friday of this week. This will be _____ final game of the season. Each girl must have a signed consent form for a field trip from _____ mother or father."

7. Instructions on an application for admission to a university said: "Each student must submit _____ application by December 1st. The admissions committee will render _____ final decision before April 1st."

▶ **Practice 5. Reflexive pronouns.** (Chart 8-4)
Complete the sentences with appropriate reflexive pronouns.

1. In our creative writing class, we all had to write short biographies of ____*ourselves*____.

2. Anna wrote a biography of _____.

3. Tom wrote a biography of _____.

4. Larry and Harry, who are twins, wrote biographies of _____, but surprisingly, they were not similar.

5. I wrote a biography of _____.

6. After our teacher had read them all, he asked us, "Did all of you enjoy writing about _____?"

7. One student replied. He said, "Well, yes, I think we did. But now we would like to know something about you. Will you tell us about _____?"

▶ **Practice 6. Reflexive pronouns.** (Chart 8-4)
Complete the sentences with one of the words or phrases from the list, and add a reflexive pronoun.

| feeling sorry for | help | ✓ is angry at | pat |
| fix | introduce | laugh at | talks to |

1. John overslept and missed his plane to San Francisco. Now he ____*is angry at himself*____ for not checking his alarm clock before going to bed.

2. I didn't know anyone at the party. I stood alone for a while; then I decided to walk over to an interesting-looking person and _____ to him.

3. Sue, please _____ to some more cake. And would you like some more coffee?

4. You did a great job, team. You should all _____ on the back for playing the game so well.

5. Sabrina is a lonely little girl. She doesn't have any brothers or sisters, or live near any friends. Sometimes she _____ or to an imaginary friend.

6. The sink is not going to _____. We have to call a plumber to repair it.

7. Come on, Kim. Don't be so hard on yourself. Everyone makes mistakes. We have to _____ sometimes and keep a sense of humor!

8. I told Tommy he couldn't buy a new toy today. He's mad at me. He's in his bedroom _____ .

▶ **Practice 7. Using *you, one,* and *they* as impersonal pronouns.** (Chart 8-5)
Choose the correct pronoun to complete each sentence. Write the letter of the pronoun.

1. People make New Year's resolutions at the beginning of a new year. They promise _____ that they will do something to improve their well-being, or to benefit their community or the world.
   a. them   b. oneself   c. themselves

2. One should be honest with _____.
   a. one   b. oneself   c. yourself

3. Parents tell their children, "You should be polite to _____ elders."
   a. your   b. one's   c. their

4. How do _____ start this car?
   a. you   b. one   c. he

5. How does _____ make a complaint in this store? Is there a customer-service department?
   a. you   b. they   c. one

6. If you are a student, _____ can get a discount at shops in the mall.
   a. they   b. you   c. one

7. Students can get discounts at the mall. _____ just have to show their student ID.
   a. They   b. Themselves   c. One

▶ **Practice 8. Forms of *other.*** (Chart 8-6)
Complete each sentence. Write the letter of the correct form of *other*.

1. One of the biggest problems in the world is global warming. _____ problem is AIDS.
   a. Another   b. The another   c. Other

2. Some cities have strict anti-pollution laws, but _____ cities do not.
   a. other   b. others   c. the others

3. New York is a multilingual city. In addition to English, many people speak Spanish. _____ speak French, Chinese, Portuguese, or Russian.
   a. Others   b. Other   c. Another

4. In addition to these languages, there are 40 _____ languages spoken in New York City, according to the U.S. Census Bureau.
   a. other   b. others   c. another

5. Istanbul lies on both sides of the Straits of Bosporus. One side is in Europe, and _____ side is in Asia.
   a. another   b. the other   c. other

6. There are 47 countries in Africa. Of these, 35 countries have coastlines. _____ do not have coastlines; they are landlocked.
   a. Others   b. The other   c. The others

7. There are several countries that have a king or a queen. One is Thailand. _____ is England.
   a. Another   b. The other   c. The another

8. There are a few _____ countries that have a king or a queen, but I can't remember which ones.
   a. others   b. other   c. another

9. Scandinavia consists of four countries. One is Denmark. _____ are Finland, Norway, and Sweden.
   a. The other   b. The others   c. Others

10. Canada has ten provinces. French is the official language of Quebec province. English is the language of _____ provinces.
    a. others   b. another   c. the other

11. Washington is one of the five states of the United States with borders on the Pacific Ocean. What are _____ states?*
    a. other   b. the other   c. the others

▶ **Practice 9. Forms of *other*.** (Chart 8-6)
Circle the correct word or phrase.

1. A: How much longer until we get home?
   B: We're almost there. We have (*other* / *another*) twenty minutes.

2. A: This road is expensive! I see we have to pay more money at the next toll booth.
   B: Right. I think we have to pay (*another* / *others*) three dollars.

3. A: So you didn't buy that house way out in the country?
   B: No, it's too far from work. I have to drive ten miles to work now. I don't want to add (*another* / *the another*) ten miles to the trip.

4. A: I heard you moved out of your apartment.
   B: That's right. They raised the rent by 100 euros. I didn't want to pay (*other* / *another*) 100 euros.

5. A: How was the test?
   B: I am sure that I failed. I didn't finish. I needed (*the other* / *another*) ten or fifteen minutes to finish.

6. A: Who won the game?
   B: The other team. In the last minute of the game, our team scored six points, not enough to win; we needed (*another* / *other*) eight points.

---

*See the Answer Key for the answer to this question.

▶ **Practice 10. Common expressions with *other*.** (Chart 8-7)
Complete the sentences in Column A with a phrase from Column B.

Column A

1. John loves Mary and Mary loves John. They love ____.

2. Nobody in my class understands this poem ____ Ron, who seems to understand everything.

3. The discussion group doesn't meet every week; it meets ____ week, that is, twice a month.

4. A tiger is a feline; ____, it's a cat, a big cat.

5. The children jumped into the water one by one, in a line, one ____.

6. What? The letter carrier quit his job? I saw him just ____. He seemed happy.

Column B

a. every other
b. after another
c. the other day
d. each other
e. in other words
f. other than

▶ **Practice 11. Nouns and pronouns.** (Chapters 6 → 8)
Correct the errors. The first paragraph has 4 errors. The second paragraph has 12 errors. The third paragraph has 13 errors.

(1) The potatoes are grown in most country. They are one of the most widely grown vegetable in the world. They are very versatile; they can be prepared in many different way.

(2) French fry are popular almost everywhere. Besides frying it, you can boil or bake potato. Other way people use potatoes is to make potato flour for bread and another kinds of dishes. Its also possible to make alcoholic beverages from potato. There are still others ways potatoes are used by commercial food processor to make product such as potatoes chips and freeze-dried potato.

(3) Potato originated in South America, where it were cultivated by the Incas as early as 5,000 year ago. It is believed that potatoes were the worlds first freeze-dried food. Over 4,000 years ago, the Incas carried his harvested potato up into the mountains and spread them on the ground to freeze overnight. The next day, after sun came up and heated the potatoes, the Incas squeezed the water out of them by stepping on it. This process were repeated for four or five day until almost all the moisture was gone from the potatoes. The Incas then dried the potatoes and stored it in pot. An Indians of South America still do this today.

Chapter 9
Modals, Part 1

▶ **Practice 1. Basic modal introduction.** (Chart 9-1)
Correct the errors in verb forms. Not all sentences have errors.

1. He can ~~to~~ hear it.
2. He can hear it.
3. He can heard it.
4. Can you help me?
5. Do you can help me?
6. They can't help me.
7. He oughts to help you.
8. He is able to help you.
9. He supposed to help you.
10. They have to do it.
11. We have got to do it.
12. She should to tell the truth.

▶ **Practice 2. Polite requests with "I" as the subject; polite requests with "you" as the subject.** (Charts 9-2 and 9-3)
Complete the sentences with a phrase from the list. Write the letter of the phrase that fits the sentence.

a. Can I help you
b. Can you hurry
c. could you help me
d. Could you please repeat
e. May I borrow
f. Would you please give me

1. A: Omigosh! I've lost my passport. Rick, _____ find it?

   B: OK. I'll be right there.

2. A: Omigosh! I've lost my passport.

   B: _____, Jenny? Maybe I can find it for you.

3. A: I'm sorry. Mr. Robbins isn't in today. Do you want to leave a message on his voice mail?

   B: Well, it's very important. _____ his cell phone number?

4. A: _____ your dictionary, please?

   B: Sure.

5. A: OK, sir. I'll be there some time today to fix your refrigerator.

   B: _____, please? All the food is melting fast!

6. A: Students, do you understand the assignment?

   B: Not really, Dr. Johnson. _____ what you said?

► **Practice 3. Polite requests with *Would you mind.*** (Chart 9-4)

Complete the sentences with *if I* + the present tense or the *-ing* form of the verb.

1. a. I want you to cook dinner.   Would you mind _____*cooking*_____ dinner?

   b. I want to cook dinner.   Would you mind _____*if I cooked*_____ dinner?

2. a. We want you to take us to the airport.   Would you mind _____ us to the airport?

   b. We want to take you to the airport.   Would you mind _____ you to the airport?

3. a. I want to open the windows.   Would you mind _____ the windows?

   b. I want you to open the windows.   Would you mind _____ the windows?

4. a. We want you to join us for lunch.   Would you mind _____ us for lunch?

   b. We want to join you for lunch.   Would you mind _____ you for lunch?

5. a. I want you to write a letter to the boss.   Would you mind _____ a letter to the boss?

   b. I want to write a letter to the boss.   Would you mind _____ a letter to the boss?

► **Practice 4. Polite requests with *Would you mind.*** (Chart 9-4)

Complete the sentences with the verbs in parentheses. Write *if I* + the past tense or the *-ing* form of the verb. In some sentences, either response is possible, but the meaning is different.

1. A: It's cold in here. Would you mind (*close*) _____*closing*_____ the window?
   B: Not at all. I'd be glad to.

2. A: It's cold in here. Would you mind (*close*) _____*if I closed*_____ the window?
   B: Not at all. Go right ahead. I think it's cold in here too.

3. A: You're going to the library? Would you mind (*take*) _____ this book back to the library for me?
   B: Not at all.

4. A: I'm not feeling well at all. Would you mind (*go*) _____ home now?
   B: Oh, I'm sorry. I hope you can come back when you feel better.

5. A: I'm not feeling well at all. Would you mind (*leave*) _____ now before the visiting hours are over?
   B: Oh, of course not. We shouldn't stay more than a short time for a hospital visit anyway.

6. A: I'll be working late tonight, honey. Would you mind (*cook*) _____ dinner tonight? I'll clean up after dinner.
   B: I'd be happy to. About what time do you think you'll be home?

7. A: We have a lot of chicken left over from dinner last night. Would you mind (*make*) _____ a chicken salad from the leftovers for dinner tonight?

   B: No, that'll be good. You make a great chicken salad.

8. A: I'm feeling kind of worn out. Chopping wood in the hot sun is hard on me. Would you mind (*finish*) _____ the work yourself?

   B: No problem, Grandpa. Why don't you go in and rest? I'll finish up.

9. A: Would you mind (*use*) _____ your name as a reference on this job application?

   B: Not at all. In fact, ask them to call me.

10. A: I'd like to apply for the job as department manager. Would you mind (*recommend*) _____ me to the boss?

    B: No. As a matter of fact, I was thinking of recommending you myself.

▶ **Practice 5. Expressing necessity, lack of necessity, and prohibition.**
(Charts 9-5 and 9-6)

Read the statements. Then check the box that describes each item.

	Necessity	Lack of Necessity	Prohibition
1. Taxpayers must pay their taxes by April 15th.			
2. You must not touch electrical wires.			
3. Students don't have to register on campus. They can register by computer.			
4. We've got to hurry! We don't want to miss our flight!			
5. You don't have to pay for the car all at once. You can pay month by month.			
6. Passengers must show their boarding passes and their IDs when they go through security.			
7. A person has to be seventeen years old to obtain a driver's license in many states.			
8. Doctors have to graduate from medical school and pass special exams before they can practice medicine.			
9. Soldiers must not disobey a superior officer.			
10. Nobody has to come to work tomorrow! The company has given everybody a day off.			

▶ **Practice 6. Past tense of *must* and *have to*.** (Chart 9-5)
Rewrite the sentences using the past tense.

1. I must be on time for my job interview.

   _____

2. The students have to memorize 100 new words a week.

   _____

3. Sylvia has to cancel her summer vacation. She has too much work to do.

   _____

4. Who do you have to call?

   _____

5. The children must get vaccinations.

   _____

6. The passengers have to fasten their seat belts because of the turbulent weather.

   _____

▶ **Practice 7. Expressing necessity and prohibition.** (Charts 9-5 and 9-6)
Write the letter of the correct word or phrase.

1. Plants _____ have water in order to live.
   a. must   b. don't have to   c. must not

2. A lot of people _____ leave their homes to go to work. They can work from their home offices.
   a. must   b. don't have to   c. must not

3. To stay alive, people _____ breathe oxygen.
   a. must   b. don't have to   c. must not

4. People who have diabetes will have serious health problems if they eat foods with a lot of sugar.
   They _____ eat foods with a lot of sugar.
   a. must   b. don't have to   c. must not

5. A salesperson _____ motivate people to buy his/her product.
   a. has to   b. doesn't have to   c. must not

6. You _____ finish your work on this project before you go on vacation. Your job is at risk.
   a. must   b. must not   c. don't have to

7. My room is a mess, but I _____ clean it before I go out tonight. I can do it in the morning.
   a. have got to   b. must not   c. don't have to

8. I _____ get some help with my statistics course. If I don't, I won't pass it.
   a. have got to   b. must not   c. don't have to

9. Yoko _____ study for her English tests. She understands everything without studying.
   a. has to   b. must not   c. doesn't have to

10. Everywhere in the world, stealing is against the law. People _____ steal.
    a. must   b. must not   c. don't have to

▶ **Practice 8. Verb form review: *have to*.** (Charts 9-5 and 9-6)
Complete the sentences with an appropriate form of *have to*. Include any words in parentheses.

1. Richard travels to Russia on business frequently. Luckily, he speaks Russian, so he

   (*not*) _____ rely on an interpreter when he's there.

2. Jackie _____ go to an important meeting in Sydney last month.

3. I (*not*) _____ water the garden later today. Joe has agreed to do it for me.

4. I _____ write three term papers for my history class last semester.

5. Matt has been nearsighted all his life. He _____ wear glasses even when he was

   a child.

6. In your country, _____ children _____ attend school?

7. Years ago, there weren't laws to keep children in school. If poor families needed the money,

   children _____ work to contribute income to the family. Children

   (*not*) _____ stay in school in those days.

8. High school graduates (*not*) _____ attend college, but of course,

   many want to.

9. Anyone who wants to drive a truck _____ get a special truck driver's license.

10. A: You're leaving so early!

    B: Yes. I'm sorry. I _____ finish some work for tomorrow before I go to bed

    tonight.

▶ **Practice 9. Advisability: *should, ought to, had better*.** (Chart 9-7)
Which sentence in each pair has a stronger meaning? Circle the letter.

1. a. I should study.
   b. I'd better study.

2. a. You must turn right here.
   b. You should turn right here.

3. a. He's got to get a warmer jacket.
   b. He ought to get a warmer jacket.

4. a. You should get new tires for your car.
   b. You'd better get new tires for your car.

5. a. They shouldn't say those words.
   b. They must not say those words.

6. a. Jane had better not tell anyone about this.
   b. Jane shouldn't tell anyone about this.

7. a. You must not drink the water here.
   b. You shouldn't drink the water here.

8. a. We don't have to vote for John Turner.
   b. We shouldn't vote for John Turner.

▶ **Practice 10. Advisability: *should, ought to, had better*.** (Chart 9-7)
Cross out the ideas that are not good advice for each situation, or are not relevant to the situation.

1. José wants to lose weight.
   a. He should exercise regularly.
   b. ~~He should eat a lot of sweets.~~
   c. He should go on a diet.

2. Ludmila wants to go to medical school in a few years.

   a. She should study poetry now.
   b. She should take science and math courses now.
   c. She should start saving money for tuition.

3. Ikira is a concert pianist.

   a. He should take good care of his hands.
   b. He should go bowling often.
   c. He should visit his grandmother often.

4. Mia is failing her math class.

   a. She should drink a lot of black coffee.
   b. She should get a tutor to help her.
   c. She should study more.

5. Beth wants her flowers to grow.

   a. She should water them.
   b. She should take any weeds out of her garden.
   c. She should give the flowers plant food as directed.

6. Ira sprained his ankle.

   a. He should practice standing on it.
   b. He should rest his ankle.
   c. He should put ice on it.

▶ **Practice 11. *Should, ought to, had better.*** (Chart 9-7)
Give advice to the people in the following situations. Write the letter of the piece of advice that fits each situation.

   a. call home and talk to his family quite often
   b. change his clothes before he goes
   c. clean it up right away
   d. get his roommate a set of earphones
   e. join some clubs to meet people with similar interests
   f. make her own decisions about her career
   g. stop for gas as soon as we see a station
   h. take it back now so you won't have to pay any more money

1. Ann would like to make some new friends. She should ____.

2. We're running out of gas! We had better ____.

3. Sam and Tim, both teenagers, have messed up the house, and their parents are coming home

   soon. They had better ____.

4. You are going to have to pay a fine because your library book is overdue. You ought to ____.

5. Ron is wearing jeans. He has to go to a formal reception this evening. He had better ____.

6. Mary's parents expect her to work in the family business, a shoe store, but she is an adult and

   wants to be an architect. She should ____.

7. Richard's roommate, Charlie, stays up very late studying. While Charlie is studying, he listens

   to loud music, and Richard can't get to sleep. Richard ought to ____.

8. Pierre is feeling really homesick these days. He should ____.

► **Practice 12. The past form of *should*.** (Chart 9-8)

Give advice about the situation using the past form of *should*. Complete each sentence with a verb from the list. Use any words in parentheses.

buy	come	order	take	visit
change	keep	stay	turn	watch

1. A: We're having hamburgers? I thought you were cooking a turkey for the holiday.

   B: Well, I did, but I cooked it for too long. It burned up in the oven! I _____ it out after three hours, but I forgot.

2. A: Where are we? Are we lost?

   B: I think we are. We _____ left instead of right at the last intersection.

3. A: I'm tired this morning! What time did we finally go to bed last night?

   B: Around 2:00 A.M. We (*not*) _____ that late movie.

4. A: Is Lionel angry at you?

   B: He is. I _____ his mother when she was so sick, but I didn't.

5. A: Beautiful shoes! Where did you buy them?

   B: I bought them at Norwalk's, but I _____ them at Pansy's Discount Store. They were a lot cheaper there.

6. A: How was dinner at Henri's?

   B: Not so good. I had the fish, but it didn't taste fresh. I _____ something else.

7. A: Why are you upset with Frank?

   B: He came to work today with his terrible cold, coughing and sneezing all over us! He (*not*) _____ to work today. He _____ home.

8. A: Are you glad you took the new job?

   B: No, actually, I'm not. I (*not*) _____ jobs. I _____ my old job.

► **Practice 13. Present and past forms of *should*.** (Charts 9-7 and 9-8)

Give advice in each situation. Complete each sentence with the present or past form of *should* and the verb in parentheses.

1. Travel broadens one's horizons. Everyone (*travel*) _____ .

2. We did not travel to Africa when we had the opportunity last year. We (*go*) _____ _____ at that time.

3. Our house will look much better with a fresh coat of paint. It will look good in a yellow color. I think we (*paint*) _____ our house, and the color (*be*) _____ yellow.

4. We painted our house. Now it's white and has beige shutters. It doesn't look good. We (*not, paint*) _____ our house in such dull colors.

5. Ernie is allergic to shellfish. Last night he ate shellfish, and he broke out with terrible hives. Ernie (*not, eat*) _____ that shellfish.

6. Some people are sensitive to caffeine. They cannot fall asleep at night if they drink coffee in the afternoon. These people (*not, drink*) _____ coffee after 12:00 P.M. They (*drink*) _____ decaffeinated coffee or tea instead.

7. Years ago, people did not realize that some species were dying off because of human activity. For example, many buffalo in North America were killed because of human thoughtlessness. As a result, there are few buffalo left in North America. People (*not, kill*) _____ those buffalo.

8. Today, people are making efforts to save the environment and to save endangered species. We (*make*) _____ strong efforts to recycle, conserve our resources, and nourish endangered species.

▶ **Practice 14. Obligation: *be supposed to.*** (Chart 9-9)

Rewrite the sentences. Use a form of ***be supposed to*** + verb.

1. Allen is expected to arrive at seven o'clock. Will he?
   Allen _____ at seven o'clock. Will he?

2. I'm expected to go hiking with Beth on Saturday, but I'd really rather sleep late.
   I _____ hiking with Beth on Saturday, but I'd really rather sleep late.

3. The weather is expected to be nice over the weekend.
   It _____ nice over the weekend.

4. The plane was expected to arrive at 6:35, but it didn't.
   The plane _____ at 6:35, but it didn't.

5. I was expecting my friends to come over tonight, but they didn't.
   They _____ tonight, but they didn't.

6. Our dog is very independent. We expect him to run to us when we call his name, but he completely ignores us.
   Our dog _____ to us when we call his name, but he completely ignores us.

▶ **Practice 15. Unfulfilled intentions: *was / were going to.*** (Chart 9-10)
Circle *yes* if the sentence expresses intention. Circle *no* if not.

		Expresses Intention	
1.	We are going to visit our cousins on Saturday.	yes	no
2.	We were going to visit our cousins on Saturday, but Jack got sick.	yes	no
3.	Ann was going down the stairs when she fell down and sprained her ankle.	yes	no
4.	I had planned to finish writing this document tonight, but I couldn't.	yes	no
5.	I was going to finish writing this document tonight, but I can't.	yes	no
6.	I was just finishing the document when my computer crashed.	yes	no
7.	I had planned to wash my car, but it rained.	yes	no
8.	I was going to wash my car, but it rained.	yes	no
9.	I was washing my car when it began to rain.	yes	no
10.	I was going to the car wash when it began to rain.	yes	no

▶ **Practice 16. Obligation: *be supposed to* and unfulfilled intentions: *was / were going to.*** (Charts 9-9 and 9-10)
Complete the sentences with a logical phrase from the list. Write the letter of the phrase.

a. he'll be late
b. I didn't want to upset you
c. I fell asleep
d. it's already two hours late
e. she lost her voice

f. the audience was applauding wildly
g. the bus broke down
h. the weather report was terrible
i. there was no lettuce in the fridge
j. they saw a train wreck

1. The plane was supposed to arrive at noon, but _____.
2. The students were going to go by bus to the TV station, but _____.
3. Tim was supposed to be here by 6:00, but _____.
4. The students were going by bus to the TV station when _____.
5. I was going to tell you the bad news, but _____.
6. Elena was going to sing at the concert, but _____.
7. Jenny was singing at the concert, and _____.
8. I was planning to watch the movie from beginning to end, but _____.
9. Dan was going to make a salad, but _____.
10. We were going to go sailing last weekend, but _____.

▶ **Practice 17. Making suggestions: *could* vs. *should.*** (Chart 9-12)
Write ***could*** or ***should*** as appropriate.

1. PATIENT: I don't know what to do about my noisy neighbors. They play their music so loud that it's driving me crazy.

   PSYCHOLOGIST: Well, you _____ play your own music louder, or you _____ call the police.

   PATIENT: No, seriously. I don't like those ideas. I want you to give me some good advice.

PSYCHOLOGIST: OK, if you insist. Then I think you _____ try to talk to them about the situation in a nonthreatening manner. That's the best way.

PATIENT: I agree. That's exactly what I _____ do, and I will.

2. WAITER: Good evening. My name is Walter, and I'll be your server tonight.

CARL: Good evening. What kind of fish is fresh tonight?

WAITER: The snapper is excellent. It's the best.

CARL: Well, I _____ order snapper, but . . . do you have wild salmon? I _____ order that, perhaps, or . . . .

WAITER: The snapper is out of this world. You _____ have the snapper.

CARL: OK, if you say that I _____ have the snapper, I will take your advice. I'll have the snapper with lemon and garlic.

3. SAM: The bridge is closed for repairs. How can we get across the lake into the city?

MARY: Well, you _____ take the Lincoln Bridge — that's five miles south of here, or you _____ drive north about fifteen miles and take the Longman Tunnel.

BOB: No, no, those routes are too long and not scenic. Here's what you _____ do, Sam: You _____ drive north for about thirty miles, and head east. You'll be entirely north of the lake then, and you won't need a bridge.

▶ **Practice 18. Chapter review.**
Correct the modal verb errors.

1. Our teacher can to speak five languages.

2. Oh, this table is heavy! Jim, may you help me move it?

3. We come to class on weekdays. We are not have to come to class on weekends.

4. Park here. It's free. You must not pay anything.

5. When you speak in court, you must to tell the truth. You must not tell lies.

6. Pat looks tired. She should gets some rest.

7. I wanted tickets for the concert, but they were all sold out. I should ordered them sooner.

8. The children are suppose to be in bed by nine o'clock.

9. The Garcias supposed to be here at 7:00, but I think they will be late, as usual.

10. We're going to make chicken for dinner. Why you don't join us?

11. Here's my advice about your diet, Mr. Jackson. You could not eat a lot of sugar and salt.

12. A: This is wonderful music. Will we dance?

    B: No, let's don't dance. Let's just sit here and talk.

Chapter 10
Modals, Part 2

▶ **Practice 1. Degrees of certainty: *must* and *may / might / could.*** (Chart 10-1)
How certain is the speaker when making each of the following remarks? Check the appropriate box.

	100%	About 95%	About 50% or less
1. Charlotte might be home by now.			
2. Phil must be home now.			
3. Mr. Brown's at home now.			
4. Lilly must know the answer to this question.			
5. Fred might have the answer.			
6. Shelley knows the answer.			
7. Those people must have a lot of money.			
8. You may remember me from high school.			
9. We could be related!			
10. Traffic might be heavy on the interstate.			

▶ **Practice 2. Degrees of certainty: *must* and *may / might / could.*** (Chart 10-1)
Circle the letter of the correct word to complete each sentence. In some sentences, both are correct.

1. A: Drive slowly! This is a school zone. Children are crossing the street here.

   B: It _____ be three o'clock. That's the time that school is out.

       a. must   b. might

2. A: Professor McKeon says that we're going to have a very high inflation rate next year.

   B: He _____ be right. He knows more about economics than anyone I know.

       a. must   b. could

3. A: Have you heard anything from Ed? Is he still on safari in Africa?

   B: He _____ be, or he _____ already be on his way home. I'm just not sure.

       a. must . . . must   b. may . . . may

4. A: Is that a famous celebrity over there in the middle of that crowd?

   B: It _____ be. She's signing autographs.

       a. must   b. might

5. A: Isn't Peter Reeves a banker?

   B: Yes. Why don't you talk to him? He _____ be able to help you with your loan.

       a. must   b. may

6. A: Is Margaret's daughter sixteen yet?

   B: She _____ be. I saw her driving a car, and you have to be at least sixteen to get a driver's license.

       a. must   b. might

7. A: Overall, don't you think the possibility of world peace is greater now than ever before?

   B: It _____ be. I don't know. Political relationships can be fragile.

       a. must   b. may

8. A: What's the matter with my son, doctor? Why does he cough and sneeze every day?

   B: He's allergic to something. It _____ dust in the house, or certain foods, or pollen in the air, or something else. It's hard to know, so we'll do some tests to find out.

       a. must be   b. may be

9. A: The speedometer on my car is broken. Do you think I'm driving over the speed limit?

   B: I can't tell. It doesn't seem like it, but you _____.

       a. must be   b. could be

10. A: You've been on the go all day. Aren't you exhausted?

    B: Yes, I _____. I can't remember when I've ever been this worn out.

        a. am   b. must be

11. A: I thought this movie was a comedy!

    B: Me too, but it _____ sad. Look at the people leaving the theater. A lot of them are crying.

        a. might be   b. must be

12. A: How old do you think Roger is?

    B: I just saw his driver's license. He _____ 33.

        a. could be   b. is

▶ **Practice 3. Degrees of certainty: present time negative.** (Chart 10-2)
Complete the sentences with the correct phrase from the list. Write the letter of the phrase.

    a. can't be him   d. may not speak
    b. can't be true   e. must not get
    c. may not be   f. must not like

1. A: I can't hear the singers! That man sitting behind us is snoring in his sleep!

   B: I hear him! He _____ opera.

2. A: Look! Isn't that our history professor over there? In the yellow sweater!

   B: No, that _____. He's in Tokyo this week, giving a presentation.

3. A: This coffee doesn't taste very good. It's supposed to be 100 percent Arabica.

   B: It _____ 100 percent Arabica. Maybe they mixed it with something else. Maybe it's a blend.

4. A: Who is that woman standing alone over there? She isn't talking to anyone.

   B: Well, she _____ any English. Or maybe she's very shy. Anyway, let's go over and try to talk to her.

5. A: Jane has been accepted at Harvard, I heard.

   B: No way! That _____. She isn't even a good student.

6. A: Did you see the new pickup truck that Mario's driving?

   B: I sure did. It's very big. It _____ good gas mileage.

▶ **Practice 4. Degrees of certainty: past time.** (Chart 10-3)
Which sentence describes the given sentences? Circle the correct letter.

1. The little boy is crying. His knees are scraped and bleeding.
   a. He may have fallen down.
   b. He must have fallen down.

2. Someone called, but I don't know who it was. Maybe it was Alice, but I'm not sure.
   a. It may have been Alice.
   b. It must have been Alice.

3. Nobody's answering the phone at Juan's apartment. I guess he has already left for the airport. He always likes to get to the airport early, you know.
   a. He might have already left for the airport.
   b. He must have already left for the airport.

4. I've lost track of my old friend Lola from high school. Maybe she moved away. Maybe she got married and has a different last name.
   a. She could have moved away.
   b. She must have moved away.

5. Irv looks unhappy today. Maybe his boss criticized him. Maybe he had an argument with his girlfriend. Maybe he lost a lot of money in the stock market.
   a. Irv might have had an argument with his girlfriend.
   b. Irv must have had an argument with his girlfriend.

6. I told Charles — only Charles — about my secret engagement, but now everyone is congratulating me! It's clear that Charles can't keep a secret.
   a. Charles may have told everyone.
   b. Charles must have told everyone.

▶ **Practice 5. Degrees of certainty: past time negative.** (Chart 10-3)
Write the past negative of an appropriate modal and the verb in parentheses.

1. ANN: I've called Howard ten times, I'm sure. He doesn't answer his cell phone.

   SAM: He (*remember*) _____ you were going to call him.

   He's a little forgetful, you know. I'll bet he forgot to turn his phone on.

2. LAWYER: Mr. Jones, where were you on the night of June 24th?

   MR. JONES: I was at home. I was at home all night.

   LAWYER: You (*be*) _____ at home on that night, Mr.

   Jones. Four witnesses saw you at the victim's apartment.

3. JIM: Look! There are lights on in the Thompsons' house. Didn't they go away on vacation?

   ANN: They (*leave*) _____ yet. Or maybe they left the

   automatic timer on to deter burglars.

4. BOB: Hey, you guys! You are not supposed to ride your bikes on the sidewalk! You could

   crash into someone!

   SUE: They (*hear*) _____ you, Bob. Look! They just kept

   going.

5. Scientists are not sure why the Mayan civilization collapsed. The Mayans (*have*)

   _____ enough to eat, or perhaps their enemies became too

   strong for them.

6. After his voyage on the *Kon Tiki,* Thor Heyerdahl set forth the theory that modern Polynesians

   descended from ancient South Americans. However, later scientists believe this (*happen*)

   _____. They believe it was impossible because of recent

   DNA evidence to the contrary.

▶ **Practice 6. Degrees of certainty: present and past time.** (Charts 10-1 → 10-3)
Complete the dialogues with ***must*** and the verb in parentheses. Use the correct present or past
form. Use ***not*** if necessary.

1. A: You got here in twenty minutes! You (*drive*) _____ really fast.

   Normally it's a forty-minute drive.

   B: No faster than usual.

2. A: Sally gave a speech at her graduation. I think I saw tears in her parents' eyes.

    B: Oh, that is touching. They (*be*) _____ very proud of her.

3. A: That's strange. Oscar didn't come to the meeting. He never misses a meeting.

    B: He (*know*) _____ about it. He was out of town all last week,

    and probably no one told him.

4. A: How old do you think our teacher is?

    B: Well, she was a couple of years ahead of my father in college, so she (*be*) _____

    _____ around 55 now.

5. A: Uh-oh! I can't find my credit card.

    B: You (*leave*) _____ it at the cash register at the grocery store.

6. A: Have you seen Clark? I can't find him anywhere.

    B: He was feeling terrible. He (*go*) _____ home a while ago.

7. A: Look! Do you see that big bird on top of the tree?

    B: What big bird?

    A: You can't see that? You (*need*) _____ stronger glasses.

8. A: What happened to your knee?

    B: I twisted it very badly in the tennis match.

    A: Oh! That (*hurt*) _____ a lot!

▶ **Practice 7. *Must have* vs. *had to*.** (Charts 9-5 and 10-3)
Circle the letter of the correct response.

1. ANN: Why didn't you come to the party?
    BOB: a. I had to study.   b. I must have studied.

2. SAM: Where's Sally? She's still not here?
    DAN: a. She must have overslept.   b. She had to oversleep.

3. IRA: Thomas missed an important meeting this morning.
    JAN: I just spoke with him and he's very sick. He told me he . . .
           a. had to go to the doctor's.   b. must have gone to the
                                                doctor's.

4. BUD: We're out of coffee again.
    TOM: a. Jane must have forgotten to   b. Jane had to forget to get
             get some.   some.

5. PAT: How were you able to stay awake during that long, boring lecture?
    ONA: It was difficult!
           a. I must have drunk a lot of coffee!   b. I had to drink a lot of coffee!

6. LIL: I can't sleep again!
    MAX: a. You must have drunk too   b. You had to drink too
             much coffee today.   much coffee today.

► **Practice 8. Degrees of certainty: future time.** (Chart 10-4)
Complete the sentences in Column A with a phrase from Column B.

Column A

1. Keiko has always loved animals. She's in veterinary school now. She should _____.
2. Most apple trees bear fruit about five years after planting. Our apple tree is four years old. It should _____ next year.
3. Aunt Ella's plane arrived an hour ago. She's taking a taxi, so she should _____.
4. We could invest this money in a conservative stock fund. If we do that, we should _____ at the end of a year.
5. Ali should _____. He's been studying hard for it all semester.
6. The little horse is growing very fast. He should _____ in a year.
7. Bake the fish in the oven at 350 degrees. It should _____ in about ten minutes.
8. Take this medicine every morning. You should _____ in about two weeks.
9. Luis is taking a heavy course load. He wants to finish school quickly. He should _____.
10. The mechanic is fixing the car now. It should _____.

Column B

a. be here just in time for dinner
b. do very well on the final exam
c. feel better
d. double his weight
e. make a great veterinarian
f. have about 5 percent more
g. be fixed before five o'clock
h. graduate next June
i. be moist and tender
j. give us some apples

► **Practice 9. Degrees of certainty: future time.** (Charts 4-2, 10-1, and 10-4)
Circle the correct word.

1. Today is Monday. Tomorrow (*should / will*) be Tuesday.

2. Hello, Jack. This is Arturo in the tech department. I'm working on your computer now. Good news — I can fix it pretty easily and it (*should / must*) be ready by 5:00 P.M. today.

3. My son's birthday is next month. He (*should / will*) be two years old.

4. It's ten minutes to four. The next bus (*must / should*) arrive at four o'clock. The buses usually stop here every hour on the hour.

5. A: Don't be late! They won't let you into the theater after the play begins.

   B: OK. I (*will / should*) be at the theater at 7:15. I promise.

6. Your husband is resting comfortably, Ms. Robbins. I'm giving him some antibiotics, so the infection (*must / should*) be cleared up by next week.

7. A: Look up there. Is that Mars?

   B: I don't think so. Mars isn't visible right now. It (*should / must*) be Venus. Venus is visible now.

8. A: Who's going to win the tennis tournament?

   B: Well, the Australian is highly rated, and she (*must / should*) win, but the Serbian is good too. Maybe she'll surprise us and win.

▶ **Practice 10. Progressive forms of modals.** (Chart 10-5)
Complete the sentences. Use the appropriate progressive forms of *must*, *should*, or
may / *might* / *could* and a verb from the list. You may use a verb more than once.

date	fly	hike	kid	sleep	work

1. A: Call Phil. He's at his office now.

   B: Let's email him instead. He _____ on something important at

   the moment. Or maybe he's with a client.

2. A: When will Betty be back from Italy?

   B: Tonight. She _____ over the Atlantic at this very moment.

3. A: Helga must know the answer to this problem. Shall we call her?

   B: Not now. It's 11:00 P.M. She _____ .

4. A: Listen, I just heard this. Mr. Milner isn't going to be our teacher anymore. He has joined

   the navy.

   B: You _____! That can't be true. Who told you that?

5. A: Sara told me that she had won the lottery, and so she invited us all to dinner at Henri's

   French restaurant.

   B: Oh, she _____ when she said that. She never plays the

   lottery!

6. A: What do you think Ann's doing now on her vacation?

   B: Oh, she _____ in the mountains. Or maybe she's relaxing at

   the pool.

7. A: I was hoping to go out with John, but I heard he's dating Julia.

   B: Well, he (*not*) _____ Julia anymore. I think that they

   may have broken up.

► **Practice 11. Modals and modal phrases.** (Charts 10-1 → 10-5)
Circle the letter of the correct completion.

1. A: Where's Angie? Didn't she come back after lunch?

    B: I'm not sure where she is. But she _____ the presentation that Human Resources is giving right now.

    a. is attending   b. could attend   c. could be attending

2. A: You're taking Spanish at 8:00 A.M. every day? Why did you choose such an early class?

    B: Because Ms. Cardenas is the teacher. She _____ excellent. I've been in the class for a month now, and I don't mind the early hour.

    a. should be   b. must be   c. is

3. A: The meteorologists predicted five major hurricanes for this hurricane season.

    B: They _____ wrong, you know. Sometimes they make mistakes.

    a. must be   b. might be   c. are

4. A: Is this chicken in the refrigerator still good?

    B: I don't think so. It's been in there for over a month! It _____ spoiled by now.

    a. may be   b. must be   c. could be

5. A: Can you tell me if Flight 86 is on time?

    B: It is on time, sir. It _____ at Gate B21 in about five minutes.

    a. might arrive   b. might be arriving   c. should be arriving

6. A: Did you know that Mike got a scholarship to State School of Engineering?

    B: Yes, I know that! I was the first one he told about it. He _____ very happy.

    a. might be   b. must be   c. is

7. A: Did you know that Li received a scholarship to the City School of Music?

    B: No, I didn't. That's great news! He _____ very happy.

    a. might be   b. must be   c. is

8. A: Who's going to win the election?

    B: It's a close call. The senator _____ with all his experience, but the opposition candidate is stronger than anyone expected.

    a. must win   b. must be winning   c. should win

9. A: Where's Harold? He's supposed to be at this meeting. Didn't Jim tell him about it?

    B: Jim _____ to tell him.

    a. must forget   b. must have forgotten   c. should have forgotten

10. A: This soup has an interesting flavor, but there's too much salt in it.

    B: Yes, it is too salty. I _____ so much salt in it.

    a. must not have put   b. shouldn't have put   c. may not have put

▶ **Practice 12. Review of modals.** (Charts 10-1 → 10-5)
Write modal sentences for the situations.

1. The plane is late, and we didn't call the airport.
   a. I expect it will arrive soon. _____It should arrive soon._____
   b. Maybe it took off late. _____It may / might / could have taken off late._____
   c. It was a good idea to call the airport, but we didn't. ___We should have called the airport.___

2. There's a package in the mail.
   a. Maybe it's for me. _____
   b. I'm sure it's for me. _____
   c. It's impossible that it's for me. _____

3. Tom didn't respond to my email.
   a. I expected him to respond. _____
   b. Maybe he didn't get it. _____
   c. I'm pretty sure he didn't get it. _____
   d. His email isn't working. It was impossible for him to get it. _____
   _____

4. There's water all over the kitchen floor.
   a. Perhaps the dishwasher is leaking. _____
   b. The dishwasher is new. It's impossible that it's the dishwasher. _____
   c. I'm pretty sure a pipe is broken. _____
   d. It's a good idea for you to call a plumber. _____
   e. It isn't necessary for us to call a plumber. _____

▶ **Practice 13. Ability: *can* and *could*.** (Chart 10-6)
Complete the sentences with *can*, *can't*, *could*, or *couldn't*.

1. Fish _____ talk.

2. My uncle was a wonderful craftsman. He made beautiful things out of wood. But he _____ read or write because he never went to school.

3. An illiterate person is someone who _____ neither read nor write.

4. I _____ get to sleep last night because it was too hot in my room.

5. Why _____ all the nations of the world just get along in peace? Why are there always wars somewhere on earth?

6. When I was younger, I _____ stay up past midnight and get up at dawn feeling refreshed and ready to go. I _____ do that any longer now that I'm middle-aged.

► **Practice 14. Repeated action in the past.** (Chart 10-7)
Complete the sentences with *would* and a verb from the list. Use the words in parentheses.

bring	fall	sleep	tell	wipe
come	listen	stay	throw	yell

1. I'll always remember Miss Emerson, my fifth-grade teacher. Sometimes a student

   _____ asleep in her class. Whenever that happened, Miss Emerson

   _____ a piece of chalk at the student!

2. My father never liked to talk on the phone. Whenever it rang, he *(always)* _____

   _____, "I'm not here!" Usually, he was only joking and _____

   to the phone when it was for him.

3. I have fond childhood memories of my Aunt Betsy. Whenever she came to visit, she

   (always) _____ me a little present.

4. Some people have strange habits. For example, my Uncle Oscar, who lived with us when I was

   a child, *(always)* _____ his plate with his napkin whenever he sat down to

   a meal.

5. When I was in college, I acquired some bad habits. I didn't study until the night before a test,

   and then I _____ up all night studying. Then the next day after the test, I

   _____ all afternoon.

6. I'll never forget the wonderful evenings I spent with my grandparents when I was a child. My

   grandmother _____ stories of her childhood seventy years ago, and we

   _____ intently and question her for every detail.

► **Practice 15. Expressing preference: *would rather*.** (Chart 10-8)
Complete the sentences with a form of *would rather* and a verb from the list. Use the words in parentheses.

eat	go	have	sail	say	study

1. I know you want to know, but I *(not)* _____ anything more

   about this topic. I told Marge that I'd keep it a secret.

2. Last night, I _____ home right after dinner at the

   restaurant, but my friends insisted on going back to John's apartment to listen to some music

   and talk.

3. I _____ history and literature in college than study

   business as I did. I majored in business, and now that's all I know. I might never again have

   the opportunity to learn about history and literature.

4. If you insist, we'll go to the pizza place after the movie, but I (*not*) _____

_____ pizza again. I'm tired of it.

5. Do you think that young people _____ a choice about whom to

marry, or do you think that they prefer their parents to choose a mate for them?

6. I like my work a lot, but my favorite thing is sailing. I love sailing. At this moment, even

though I have just been promoted to vice-president of my company, I

_____ right now instead of sitting here in my office.

▶ **Practice 16. Combining modals with phrasal modals.** (Chart 10-9)
Complete each sentence with the given words in its list. Write the words in their correct order in
the sentences.

1. to \ get \ have

You _____ a passport if you are going to travel in other countries.

2. be \ should \ to \ able \ complete

Everyone _____ this form easily.

3. have \ to \ won't \ stand

People _____ in the line for a long time. The line is

moving quickly.

4. you \ be \ able \ leave \ to \ will

When _____ here?

5. not \ able \ to \ graduate \ to \ going \ am \ be

I _____ with my class. I lost a complete

semester when I was sick.

6. been \ must \ to \ get \ have \ not \ able

Mike and Helen haven't arrived yet. They were going to try to get on an earlier flight. They

_____ on the earlier flight.

Chapter 11
The Passive

▶ **Practice 1. Forming the passive.** (Charts 11-1 and 11-2)
Change the active to the passive by writing the correct form of *be*. Use the same tense for *be* in the passive sentence that is used in the active sentence.

Example: Mrs. Bell answered my question. My question ___was___ **answered** by Mrs. Bell.

1. *simple present:*

   Authors write books. .... Books _____ **written** by authors.

2. *present progressive:*

   Mr. Brown is writing that book. .... That book _____ **written** by Mr. Brown.

3. *present perfect:*

   Ms. Lee has written the report. .... The report _____ **written** by Ms. Lee.

4. *simple past:*

   Bob wrote that letter. .... That letter _____ **written** by Bob.

5. *past progressive:*

   A student was writing the report. ..... The report _____ **written** by a student.

6. *past perfect:*

   Lucy had written a memo. .... A memo _____ **written** by Lucy.

7. *simple future:*

   Your teacher will write a report. .... A report _____ **written** by your teacher.

8. *be going to:*

   Tom is going to write a letter. .... The letter _____ **written** by Tom.

9. *future perfect:*

   Alice will have written the report. ..... The report _____ **written** by Alice.

10. The judges have made a decision. ..... A decision _____ **made** by the judges.

11. Several people saw the accident. ...The accident _____ **seen** by several people.

12. Ann is sending the letters. .... The letters _____ **sent** by Ann.

13. Fred will plan the party. .... The party _____ **planned** by Fred.

14. The medicine had cured my illness. .. My illness _____ **cured** by the medicine.

15. The cat will have caught the mouse. ..The mouse _____ **caught** by the cat.

16. Engineers design bridges. .... Bridges _____ **designed** by engineers.

17. The city is going to build a bridge. ...... A bridge _____ **built** by the city.

18. A guard was protecting the jewels. .... The jewels _____ **protected** by a guard.

▶ **Practice 2. Active vs. passive.** (Charts 11-1 and 11-2)
Underline the subject of each sentence. Circle the complete verb. Then identify the sentences as active (A) or passive (P).

1. __A__ Henry (visited) a national park.

2. __P__ The park (was visited) by over 10,000 people last month.

3. ____ Olga was reading the comics.

4. ____ Philippe has read all of Tolstoy's novels.

5. ____ *Bambi* has been read by children all over the world.

6. ____ Whales swim in the ocean.

7. ____ Whales were hunted by fishermen until recently.

8. ____ The answer won't be known for several months.

9. ____ I know the answer.

10. ____ Two new houses were built on our street.

11. ____ A famous architect designed the new bank on First Street.

12. ____ Television was invented before I was born.

13. ____ The World Cup is seen on television all over the world.

14. ____ Television has expanded the knowledge of people everywhere.

▶ **Practice 3. Forming the passive.** (Chart 11-2)
Complete the sentences. Change the verbs in *italics* from active to passive.

1. Sue *writes* the book. → The book ___is written___ by Sue.

2. Sue *is writing* the book. → The book _____ by Sue.

3. Sue *has written* the book. → The book _____ by Sue.

4. Sue *wrote* the book. → The book _____ by Sue.

5. Sue *was writing* the book. → The book _____ by Sue.

6. Sue *had written* the book. → The book _____ by Sue.

7. Sue *will write* the book. → The book _____ by Sue.

8. Sue *is going to write* the book. → The book _____ by Sue.

9. Sue *will have written* the book. › The book _____ by Sue.

10. *Did* Sue *write* the book? → _____ the book _____ by Sue?

11. *Will* Sue *write* the book? → _____ the book _____ by Sue?

12. *Has* Sue *written* the book? → _____ the book _____ by Sue?

▶ **Practice 4. Forming the passive.** (Chart 11-2)

Part I. Complete the sentences. Change the verbs from active to passive.

1. Picasso painted that picture.

   That picture ___was painted by Picasso___.

2. Experienced pilots fly these planes.

   These planes _____.

3. A famous singer is going to sing the national anthem.

   The national anthem _____.

4. Yale University has accepted my cousin.

   My cousin _____.

5. The doctor will examine the patient.

   The patient _____.

6. The defense attorney is questioning a witness.

   A witness _____.

7. A dog bit our mail carrier.

   Our mail carrier _____.

8. The mother bird was feeding the baby bird.

   The baby bird _____.

9. His words won't persuade me.

   I _____.

10. I didn't paint this picture. Did Laura paint it?

    The picture _____. Was it _____?

11. Does Mrs. Crane own this restaurant? I know that her father doesn't own it anymore.

    Is this restaurant _____?

    I know that it _____.

12. I didn't sign these papers. Someone else signed my name.

    These papers _____.

    My name _____.

Part II. Change each sentence to the active voice. The subject of the new sentence is given. Keep the same tense of the verb.

13. My teeth are going to be cleaned by the dental assistant.

    The dental assistant _____.

14. Was that email sent by Mr. Tyrol?

    _____ Mr. Tyrol _____?

15. The Fourth of July isn't celebrated by the British.

    The British _____.

16. Has your house been sold by the realtor yet?

    _____ the realtor _____?

17. The thief hasn't been caught by the police.

    The police _____.

18. The carpets are being cleaned by the carpet cleaners.

    The carpet cleaners _____.

► **Practice 5. Active vs. passive.** (Charts 11-1 and 11-2)

In these sentences, some of the verbs are transitive and some are intransitive. <u>Underline</u> the verb in each sentence. Then identify the object of the verb if there is one. If the verb has an object, change the sentence to the passive. If not, write Ø.

	Verb	Object Of Verb	Passive Sentence
1. Al <u>will pay</u> the bill.	*will pay*	*the bill*	*The bill will be paid by Al.*
2. Jane <u>will arrive</u> tomorrow.	*will arrive*	*Ø*	*Ø*
3. The hotel supplies towels.			
4. Accidents happen every day.			
5. Everyone noticed my error.			
6. The train arrived at three.			
7. The news didn't surprise me.			
8. Did the news surprise you?			
9. Do ghosts exist?			
10. Mr. Lee died last year.			
11. An old man told the story.			
12. It hasn't rained lately.			

► **Practice 6. Active vs. passive.** (Charts 11-1 and 11-2)

Complete the sentences. Write the letter of the correct verb.

1. We'll let you know about the job. You _____ by my secretary next week.
   a. will notify   b. will be notified   c. will have notified

2. Last night I _____ to lock my front door.
   a. wasn't remembered   b. didn't remember   c. hadn't been remembered

3. This old wooden chest _____ by my grandfather over 40 years ago.
   a. built   b. had built   c. was built

4. Disneyland is a world-famous amusement park in Southern California. It _____ by millions of people every year.
   a. is visited   b. visited   c. has visited

5. I _____ with people who say space exploration is a waste of money. What do you think?
   a. not agree   b. don't agree   c. am not agree

6. Do you really think that we _____ by creatures from outer space in the near future?
   a. will invade   b. be invaded   c. will be invaded

7. Had you already _____ by this university when you heard about the scholarship offer from the other school?
   a. were accepted   b. accepted   c. been accepted

8. When Alex was only ten, his father _____.
   a. was died   b. died   c. dead

9. Elephants _____ a long time, sometimes for 70 years.
   a. live   b. were lived   c. have been lived

10. The impact of the earthquake yesterday _____ by people who lived hundreds of kilometers from the epicenter.
   a. felt   b. has felt   c. was felt

11. At one time, the entire world _____ by dinosaurs.
   a. ruled   b. was ruled   c. been ruled

12. Some dinosaurs _____ on their hind legs and were as tall as palm trees.
   a. walked   b. were walked   c. have stood

▶ **Practice 7. Using the passive.** (Chart 11-3)
Circle the letter of the sentence that has the same meaning as the given sentence.

1. In my dream, the monster is being chased.
   a. The monster is chasing someone in my dream.
   b. Someone is chasing the monster in my dream.

2. An airplane was delivered to a cargo facility last week.
   a. The airplane delivered some cargo.
   b. Someone delivered the airplane.

3. Witnesses are going to be asked for information.
   a. Someone will request information from witnesses.
   b. Witnesses will request information from someone.

4. Internet access will be provided free of charge.
   a. The internet will provide access.
   b. Someone will provide internet access.

5. All of the participants have been counted.
   a. Someone has finished counting the participants.
   b. The participants have finished counting.

▶ **Practice 8. Using the passive.** (Chart 11-3)
Complete each passage with the given verbs. Write the correct form of the verb, active or passive.

1. *invent, tell*

   The sandwich _____ by John Montagu, an Englishman with the title of
   the Earl of Sandwich. In about 1762, he is reputed to have been too busy to sit down at a
   regular meal, so he _____ his cook to pack his meat inside some bread in
   order to save him time.

2. *attend, establish, give*

   Al-Azhar University in Cairo, Egypt, is one of the oldest universities in the world. It
   _____ at about the same time as the city of Cairo, in 969 A.D. The
   first lecture _____ in 975 A.D. Students (*still*) _____ the
   university today.

3. *become, kill, know, live, relate, save*

One animal that is famous in the history of the American West is

actually a bison, but it _____ by the name of *buffalo.*

The American buffalo _____ to a similar animal in

Asia, the water buffalo. Buffaloes _____ in parks and flat

grasslands. At the end of the nineteenth century, they almost

_____ extinct because thousands of them

_____ by hunters. Fortunately, they _____ by

the efforts of naturalists and the government.

4. *believe, give, like, originate, treat, use, value*

Garlic _____ in Asia over 6,000 years ago, and it

spread throughout Europe and Africa. Today, people _____

to use garlic not only for its strong flavor, but because it _____

them physical strength and good health. In ancient times, garlic _____

so highly that it _____ as money. Injuries and illnesses

_____ with garlic by the ancient Greeks. Even today, garlic

_____ to be effective by some people in lowering cholesterol and in

treating other digestive disorders.

▶ **Practice 9. Active vs. passive.** (Charts 11-1 → 11-3)
Write complete sentences with the given words. Use the simple past.

1. the chefs \ prepare \ the food _____.

2. the food \ prepare \ yesterday _____.

3. the rain \ stop _____.

4. a rainbow \ appear \ in the sky _____.

5. the documents \ send \ to you \ yesterday _____.

6. my lawyer \ send \ the documents to me _____.

7. the winner of the election \ announce \ on TV _____.

8. I \ not agree \ with you about this _____.

9. what \ happen \ yesterday _____?

10. something wonderful \ happen \ to me _____.

11. the trees \ die \ of a disease _____.

12. the trees \ kill \ by a disease _____.

13. a disease \ kill \ the trees _____.

14. I \ accept \ at the University of Chicago _____.

15. I \ recommend \ for a scholarship _____.

▶ **Practice 10. The passive form of modals and phrasal modals.** (Chart 11-4)
Circle the correct verb.

1. A language (*can't be / couldn't have been*) learned only by reading about it. You have to practice speaking it.

2. These jeans (*should be washed / should have been washed*) before you wear them. The material will be softer and more comfortable.

3. This shirt was washed in hot water, and it shrank. It (*should have washed / should have been washed*) in cold water.

4. The road is still being fixed. It is supposed (*to be finished / to finish*) by next month, but I'm not so sure it will be.

5. There's an old house for sale on Route 411. They say that George Washington visited it, so it (*must be built / must have been built*) in the 1700s.

6. Taxes (*have to pay / have to be paid*) on or before April 15th. Payments (*must be sent / must have been sent*) to the government on or before April 15th.

7. The senator has made a good point, but I disagree. May I (*permit / be permitted*) to speak now?

8. Our kitchen is old and dark. We're going to renovate it. It (*ought to be painted / ought to paint*) a light shade of green or white to make it look brighter.

▶ **Practice 11. The passive form of modals and phrasal modals.** (Chart 11-4)
Complete the sentences with the given words. Write the appropriate form, active or passive.

1. The decision (*should + make*) _____ as soon as possible.

2. We (*should + make*) _____ our decision right now, without further discussion.

3. A decision (*should + make*) _____ before now.

4. They say that Einstein (*couldn't + talk*) _____ until he was four years old.

5. I (*couldn't + talk*) _____ to Mr. Forth this morning even if I had wanted to. It would have been impossible. He is in Europe on business all this week.

6. All vehicles (*must + register*) _____ with the Department of Motor Vehicles of this state.

7. You (*must + register*) _____ your car with the Department of Motor Vehicles.

8. This bill (*have to + pay*) _____ by tomorrow. I (*had better not + send*) _____ a check by mail. It won't get there on time.

9. A: Who called?

   B: I don't know who it was. They hung up. It (*must + be*) _____ a wrong number.

10. A: Was Yuri at the party? Did you see him?

B: I didn't see him, but he (*may + be*) _____ there. There was a

huge crowd, and I didn't get to talk to many people.

▶ **Practice 12. Non-progressive passive.** (Chart 11-5)
Complete the sentences in Column A with a verb from Column B.

Column A

1. Uh-oh. I forgot my key, and the door is ____.
2. The museum isn't open today. It's ____.
3. Finally! The report I've been writing for a week is ____.
4. The TV doesn't work. It's ____.
5. Do you know where we are? I think we're ____.
6. Let's go to another restaurant. This one is too ____.
7. What happened to the cookies? They're all ____.
8. It's freezing in this room! I guess the heat isn't ____.

Column B

a. finished
b. lost
c. crowded
d. turned on
e. closed
f. gone
g. locked
h. broken

▶ **Practice 13. Non-progressive passive.** (Charts 11-5 and 11-6)
Complete each sentence with a verb from the list. Use the present tense, active or passive. Add a preposition if necessary.

bore	do	locate	marry
compose	interest	make	scare
depend			

1. Ismael _____ the history of languages. He is studying linguistics.

2. We may have a picnic on Saturday. It _____ the weather.

3. Sam _____ Salma. They have been married for 24 years.

4. Our son _____ the dark, so we keep a night light on in his room.

5. Golf _____ me. There isn't any action, and it is too slow.

6. These jeans _____ cotton. They're 100 percent organic cotton.

7. Our class is diverse. It _____ people from nine countries.

8. The Hague _____ the Netherlands.

9. We _____ this exercise now.

▶ **Practice 14. Common non-progressive passive verbs + prepositions.**
(Chart 11-6)
Circle the correct preposition.

1. Professor Wills is deeply involved (*by* / *in*) campus politics.

2. Who is qualified (*for* / *in*) this job?

3. Are you worried (*for* / *about*) your grade in this class?

4. A lot of people are interested (*in* / *about*) the astronauts in space.

5. Your last name is Mason? Are you related (*with* / *to*) Tony Mason?

6. Ann doesn't travel on planes. She's terrified (*from* / *of*) flying.

7. Mrs. Redmond? No, I'm not acquainted (*to* / *with*) her.

8. This is a wonderful book. I'll give it to you when I'm finished (*with* / *for*) it.

9. I'm bored (*in* / *with*) this movie. Can we leave?

10. Are you satisfied (*for* / *with*) our service? Let us know by email.

11. We are tired (*from* / *of*) paying rent, so we are going to buy an apartment.

12. Do you recycle? Are you committed (*to* / *by*) helping the environment?

▶ **Practice 15. Passive vs. active.** (Charts 11-1 → 11-6)
Correct the errors. One item doesn't need to be changed.

1. The plane was arrived very late.

2. Four people injured in the accident.

3. Bella is married with José.

4. People are worried with global warming.

5. Astronomers are interesting in several new meteors.

6. We were surprise by Harold's announcement.

7. Spanish is spoken by people in Mexico.

8. This road is not the right one. We lost.

9. Pat should try that new medicine. He might helped.

10. Lunch is been served in the cafeteria right now.

11. Something unusual was happened yesterday.

12. Will be fixed the refrigerator today?

13. Nobody knows how old my grandfather was when he died last year, but he must been over 100 years old. He remembers the flu epidemic of 1918.

▶ **Practice 16. The passive with *get*.** (Chart 11-7)
Complete the sentences with the correct word from the list.

crowded	elected	hungry	invited	scared
dressed	fat	hurt	lost	stopped

1. At first, we were the only people in the restaurant, but it quickly got _____.

2. We can eat soon if you're getting _____.

3. Stan followed the map closely and didn't get _____.

4. When I heard those strange sounds last night, I got _____.

5. Wake up and get _____! We have to leave in five minutes.

6. Be careful on these old steps. You could fall and get _____.

7. Lola is disappointed because she didn't get _____ to the party.

8. If children don't get any exercise, they might get _____.

9. Don't drive so fast! You could get _____ for speeding!

10. Dr. Sousa is going to get _____ to the city government.

▶ **Practice 17. Participial adjectives.** (Chart 11-8)
Circle the correct word.

1. When their team scored the winning point, the fans were (*exciting* / *excited*).

2. The football game was very (*exciting* / *excited*).

3. The news I just heard was (*shocking* / *shocked*).

4. Everyone was (*shocking* / *shocked*) by the news.

5. Our forty-mile bike ride was (*exhausting* / *exhausted*). I was (*exhausting* / *exhausted*) at the end of it.

6. This work is so (*boring* / *bored*). I'm very (*boring* / *bored*) with my work.

7. I'm really (*confusing* / *confused*). Professor Eng's explanation was (*confusing* / *confused*).

8. The ruins of the old city are very (*interesting* / *interested*).

9. Archeologists are (*interesting* / *interested*) in the ruins of the old city.

10. The experience of climbing Mount Kilimanjaro was (*thrilling* / *thrilled*). The climber's family was (*thrilling* / *thrilled*) when she returned safely.

▶ **Practice 18. Participial adjectives.** (Chart 11-8)
Write one of the given words to complete each sentence.

1. *fascinating, fascinated*

   a. Your lecture was _____.

   b. I was _____ by your lecture.

2. *exhausting, exhausted*

   a. Listening to Mrs. Wilson complain is _____.

   b. I am _____ by Mrs. Wilson's complaints.

3. *disappointing, disappointed*

   a. Your parents are _____ in your behavior.

   b. Your behavior is _____.

▶ **Practice 19. Participial adjectives.** (Chart 11-8)
Circle the letters of all the correct sentences in each group.

1. a. I am confused by these instructions.

   b. I am confusing by these instructions.

   c. These instructions are confused me.

   d. These instructions confuse me.

2. a. The history of civilization interests Professor Davis.

   b. The history of civilization is interesting to Professor Davis.

   c. The history of civilization is interested to Professor Davis.

   d. Professor Davis is interesting in the history of civilization.

3. a. I was embarrassing by all the attention.

   b. I was embarrassed by all the attention.

   c. All the attention embarrassed me.

   d. All the attention was embarrassed to me.

4. a. This is shocked news about your family.

   b. This is shocking news about your family.

   c. I was shocking by the news about your family.

   d. I was shocked by the news about your family.

5. a. Fred is boring by spectator sports.

   b. Spectator sports are boring to Fred.

   c. Fred is bored by spectator sports.

   d. Spectator sports are bored to Fred.

▶ **Practice 20. Participial adjectives.** (Chart 11-8)
Complete each sentence with the present or past participle of the given verbs.

1. There was an emergency on campus. We were not allowed to leave the buildings. The situation was very (*frustrate*) _____.

2. As a little boy, Tom's jokes were cute, but as a (*grow*) _____ man, his jokes irritate people. Both Tom and his jokes are (*irritate*) _____.

3. The invention of the (*wash*) _____ machine was a great help to households everywhere.

4. The pencil is a simple (*write*) _____ instrument.

5. The history of these people is not a (*write*) _____ one. The only history is oral.

6. This weather is (*depress*) _____. I've been (*depress*) _____ all day.

7. You're going to laugh a lot when you see that movie. The critics say that it is the most (*entertain*) _____ movie of the year.

8. Here's a well-(*know*) _____ saying: "Don't cry over (*spill*) _____ milk." It means that you shouldn't worry about mistakes that you've made in the past.

9. Here's a (*comfort*) _____ saying: "(*Bark*) _____ dogs seldom bite." It means that things that seem dangerous often turn out not to be dangerous.

10. Here's an (*inspire*) _____ saying: "(*Unite*) _____ we stand, (*divide*) _____ we fall." It means that we must stand together against an enemy in order to survive.

Index

Answer Key

CHAPTER 1: OVERVIEW OF VERB TENSES

PRACTICE 1, p. 1
1. eat
2. ate . . . visited . . . wrote
3. am talking . . . am answering
4. was looking
5. have asked
6. have been talking
7. will be
8. will be sitting
9. had eaten
10. will have eaten

PRACTICE 2, p. 2
1. 7th, 14th, 21st, 28th
2. 7th
3. 3rd
4. 2nd, 3rd, 4th
5. 10th, 11th, 12th
6. 14th and 15th
7. 7th
8. 24th

PRACTICE 3, p. 2
1. rains
2. visited
3. will win
4. is watching
5. will be flying
6. was thinking
7. will be working
8. went . . . were sleeping
9. fell . . . will help
10. are swimming

PRACTICE 4, p. 3
1. have
2. had
3. has been
4. was
5. will have been
6. have lived
7. had
8. have
9. had
10. had

PRACTICE 5, p. 3
1. have
2. has been
3. will have been
4. had
5. have
6. had
7. have been waiting
8. has
9. had

PRACTICE 6, p. 4
1. a
2. b
3. a
4. b
5. a
6. a
7. b
8. a
9. a

PRACTICE 7, p. 5
1. eats
2. ate
3. will eat / 'll eat
4. am eating / 'm eating
5. was eating
6. will be eating
7. have already eaten
8. had already eaten
9. will have already eaten
10. has been eating
11. had been eating
12. will have been eating dinner

PRACTICE 8, p. 7
1. at this time
2. in the past
3. daily habit
4. past and present
5. past only
6. in the past
7. at this time
8. in the future
9. daily habit
10. in the past

PRACTICE 9, p. 7
1. b. soon c. next week
2. a. right now
3. b. now c. right now
4. b. all day c. since Monday
5. a. now b. this week
6. b. next month c. this weekend
7. a. since 9:00 b. all day c. for two hours
8. a. last week c. yesterday
9. a. at midnight b. when we came
10. a. tomorrow c. in the morning
11. a. soon c. in a few days

PRACTICE 10, p. 8
1. a
2. a
3. b
4. a, b
5. a, b, c
6. a
7. a
8. a, c

PRACTICE 11, p. 8

1.	arriving	
2. copying		
3.		cutting
4. enjoying		
5. filling		
6. happening		
7.	hoping	
8.	leaving	
9.	making	
10.		rubbing
11. staying		
12.		stopping
13.	taking	
14.		winning
15. working		

PRACTICE 12, p. 9

1. bothered		
2.		copied
3. enjoyed		
4. fastened		
5. feared		
6.	occurred	
7.	patted	
8. played		
9. rained		
10.	referred	
11.		replied
12. returned		
13.	scared	
14.		tried
15. walked		

PRACTICE 13, p. 10

1. preferring   preferred
2. studying   studied
3. working   worked
4. offering   offered
5. kissing   kissed
6. playing   played
7. fainting   fainted
8. allowing   allowed
9. stopping   stopped
10. tying   tied
11. dying   died
12. folding   folded
13. trying   tried
14. deciding   decided
15. hopping   hopped

PRACTICE 14, p. 10

1. do you spell
2. spell
3. has
4. are you
5. am
6. lived
7. moved
8. did you grow
9. did you come
10. arrived
11. have been
12. do you like
13. am staying
14. am looking
15. have been looking
16. find
17. Have you found
18. had been looking
19. are you moving
20. give
21. will be moving
22. will have moved
23. will be

CHAPTER 2: PRESENT AND PAST; SIMPLE AND PROGRESSIVE

PRACTICE 1, p. 12

1. sets
2. is setting
3. are practicing
4. practice
5. listen
6. am listening / 'm listening
7. talk
8. are talking
9. are eating / 're eating
10. eat

PRACTICE 2, p. 12

1. fall
2. are falling
3. grows
4. are growing
5. shines
6. is shining . . . are singing
7. sings
8. reads
9. am calling

PRACTICE 3, p. 13

1. own
2. am trying / 'm trying
3. belongs
4. is sleeping
5. means
6. shrinks
7. is biting / 's biting
8. is bleeding / 's bleeding
9. am failing / 'm failing

PRACTICE 4, p. 13

1. a
2. b
3. a
4. b
5. a
6. a
7. b
8. a
9. a
10. a

PRACTICE 5, p. 14

1. a
2. b
3. b
4. a
5. b
6. a

PRACTICE 6, p. 15

Part I. changed . . . launched . . . was . . . weighed . . . took . . . ushered . . . was . . . marked

Part II.
1. T
2. F
3. T
4. F
5. T

PRACTICE 7, p. 15

Part I.
1. worked
2. listened
3. studied
4. rained

Part II.
5. broke
6. swam
7. hit

PRACTICE 8, p. 16

Group 1.
1. cost
2. shut
3. cut
4. quit

Group 2.
5. forgot
6. chose
7. took
8. gave

PRACTICE 9, p. 16

Group 3.
1. began
2. sang
3. ran
4. drank

Group 4.
5. bought
6. taught
7. won
8. lost
9. left
10. upset

PRACTICE 10, p. 17

Group 5.
1. knew
2. flew
3. did
4. saw

Group 6.
5. ran
6. came
7. became

Group 7.
8. was
9. went

Group 8.
10. dreamed / dreamt
11. learned / learnt
12. burned / burnt
13. spilled / spilt

PRACTICE 11, p. 18
1. sold   sold
2. bought   bought
3. began   begun
4. had   had
5. caught   caught
6. quit   quit
7. found   found
8. made   made
9. took   taken
10. broke   broken
11. came   come
12. lost   lost
13. slept   slept
14. built   built
15. fought   fought

PRACTICE 12, p. 19

Simple Form	Simple Past	Past Participle
1.	understood	understood
2. spend		spent
3.	let	let
4. see	saw	
5.	taught	taught
6. speak		spoken
7. go	went	
8.	paid	paid
9. forget	forgot	
10. write		written
11.	fell	fallen
12. feel		felt
13. leave	left	
14. upset		upset
15. fly	flew	

PRACTICE 13, p. 19
1. broke
2. stole
3. knew
4. heard
5. came
6. shook
7. hid
8. found
9. fought
10. ran
11. shot
12. caught

PRACTICE 14, p. 20
1. bit
2. held
3. meant
4. blew
5. quit
6. felt
7. stung
8. swam
9. paid
10. caught

PRACTICE 15, p. 21
1. spent
2. led
3. bet
4. wept
5. upset
6. split
7. sank
8. flew
9. spun
10. rang
11. chose
12. froze

PRACTICE 16, p. 21
1. called
2. were watching
3. was humming
4. met
5. saw
6. was cleaning
7. was driving . . . got
8. was blowing . . . were bending
9. were playing . . . was pulling

PRACTICE 17, p. 22
1. 2, 1
2. 2, 1
3. 1, 2
4. 2, 1
5. 1, 2
6. 2, 1
7. 1, 2
8. 2, 1

PRACTICE 18, p. 23
1. had
2. were having
3. stopped . . . fell . . . spilled
4. served . . . came
5. looked . . . was sleeping . . . was dreaming . . . was smiling
6. was working . . . exploded
7. caused . . . dropped

PRACTICE 19, p. 23
1. <u>2</u>   take . . . rains
2. <u>4</u>   was riding . . . heard
3. <u>1</u>   am riding . . . is repairing
4. <u>3</u>   rode . . . forgot
5. <u>4</u>   was having . . . crashed
6. <u>3</u>   had . . . didn't eat
7. <u>1</u>   is having
8. <u>2</u>   has
9. <u>2</u>   celebrate . . . are
10. <u>4</u>   were working . . . called
11. <u>3</u>   celebrated . . . was

PRACTICE 20, p. 24
1. is always complaining
2. is always talking
3. live
4. is forever leaving
5. are always interrupting
6. are always losing
7. play
8. are always studying

PRACTICE 21, p. 25

Across	Down
2. listening	1. went
5. think	3. studying
7. heard	4. ate
8. thinking	6. having
	7. have

CHAPTER 3: PERFECT AND PERFECT PROGRESSIVE TENSES

PRACTICE 1, p. 26

Part I.
1. has been . . . has remained . . . have estimated
2. has been increasing . . . have been growing
3. had been . . . had dropped
4. were
5. will be

Part II.
1. F
2. F
3. T
4. F
5. T

PRACTICE 2, p. 27
1. eaten
2. visited
3. worked
4. liked
5. known
6. worn
7. taken
8. gone
9. ridden
10. been

PRACTICE 3, p. 27
1. a. for
   b. for
   c. since
   d. since
   e. for
   f. since
   g. since
2. a. since
   b. for
   c. since
   d. for
   e. since
   f. since
   g. for

PRACTICE 4, p. 28
1. have already eaten
2. have won
3. have not written
4. has improved
5. has not started
6. have already swept
7. have you known
8. have made
9. have never ridden
10. Have you ever swum

PRACTICE 5, p. 29
1. the 21st of April . . . three weeks . . . April 1st . . . three weeks
2. two months ago . . . January 1st . . . two months
3. two weeks . . . February 14th
4. nine years . . . nine years . . . October, 2000

PRACTICE 6, p. 29

Answers will vary.
1. a. We have known Mrs. Jones for one month.
   b. We have known Mrs. Jones since last month.
2. a. They have lived there for (____) years.
   b. They have lived there since 2001.
3. a. I have liked foreign films since 200(____).
   b. I have liked foreign films for five years.
4. a. Jack has worked for a software company for one year.
   b. Jack has worked for a software company since last year.

PRACTICE 7, p. 30
1. is
2. has
3. is
4. is
5. has
6. is
7. has
8. is
9. has

PRACTICE 8, p. 30
1. became
2. has been
3. has been
4. has rained
5. lived
6. have lived
7. worked
8. haven't worked

PRACTICE 9, p. 30
1. knew . . . have known
2. agreed . . . have agreed
3. took . . . has taken
4. has played . . . played
5. wrote . . . has written
6. sent . . . have sent
7. has flown . . . flew
8. overslept . . . has overslept

PRACTICE 10, p. 31
1. have been talking
2. have spoken
3. has won
4. have you been sitting
5. have sat

PRACTICE 11, p. 31
1. have been playing
2. has played
3. has raised
4. has been lecturing
5. has never missed
6. has slept
7. have been flying
8. has been sleeping
9. have been searching

PRACTICE 12, p. 32
1. have never understood
2. have met
3. has been standing
4. has been painting
5. have never heard
6. have been traveling
7. has grown
8. wanted
9. have already spent
10. has been cooking

PRACTICE 13, p. 33

Sample answers
1. In 1999, Janet moved to Canada.
2. In 2000, Janet joined Lingua Schools as a teaching assistant.
3. Janet has been living / has lived in Canada since 1999.
4. Janet has been a teacher since 2001.
5. Janet has been teaching / has taught her own class since 2001.
6. Janet has been working / has worked at Lingua Schools since 2000.

PRACTICE 14, p. 33
1. <u>We had driven only two miles</u> = 1
   <u>we got a flat tire</u> = 2
2. <u>Alan told me</u> = 2
   <u>he had written a book</u> = 1
3. <u>we arrived at the airport</u> = 2
   <u>the plane had already left</u> = 1
4. <u>The dog had eaten the entire roast</u> = 1
   <u>anyone knew it was gone</u> = 2

5. <u>We didn't stand in line for tickets</u> = 2
   <u>we had already bought them by mail</u> = 1
6. <u>Carl played the guitar so well</u> = 2
   <u>he had studied with a famous guitarist</u> = 1
7. <u>the movie ended</u> = 2
   <u>everyone had fallen asleep</u> = 1
8. <u>the professor had corrected the third paper</u> = 1
   <u>he was exhausted from writing comments on the
   student's papers</u> = 2
9. <u>I had just placed an order at the store for a new
   camera</u> = 1
   <u>I found a cheaper one online</u> = 2

PRACTICE 15, p. 34
1. had not gotten
2. had not met
3. had not taken
4. had not eaten
5. had not had

PRACTICE 16, p. 34
1. b. had already finished
2. a. turned on
3. b. had burned
4. b. had never spent
5. a. helped
6. b. had never visited
7. b. had traveled

PRACTICE 17, p. 34
1. went . . . had never been . . . didn't take . . . was
2. ate . . . had never eaten
3. A: saw . . . did . . . Had you ever acted
   B: started

PRACTICE 18, p. 35
1. have been studying
2. had been studying
3. have been waiting
4. had been waiting
5. had been working
6. has been working

PRACTICE 19, p. 35
1. had been listening . . . have been dancing . . . singing
2. have been waiting
3. had been waiting
4. has been training
5. had been running
6. had been trying . . . has been teaching
7. has been performing
8. have been working . . . had been building

PRACTICE 20, p. 36
1. I've **seen** it ten times.
2. I've **been** reading it . . .
3. Our guests **left** . . .
4. We **have been** studying . . . .
5. I've **been** having . . .
6. . . . **had** eaten.
7. . . . , so I **ran** . . .
8. She **left** . . .
9. . . . , I **had** celebrated . . .
10. B: . . . I **have been** holding for more than half an hour!

CHAPTER 4: FUTURE TIME

PRACTICE 1, p. 37
1. He **will** be
2. will **stay** open
3. **will be**

4. Correct.
5. Our teacher **won't be**
6. Correct.

PRACTICE 2, p. 37
1. is going to visit
2. is going to win
3. are you going to take
4. is not going to be
5. Are they going to join
6. am not going to lie . . . I am going to tell

PRACTICE 3, p. 38
1. a. will set
   b. is going to set
2. a. will arrive
   b. is going to arrive
3. a. will rain
   b. is going to rain
4. a. will bloom
   b. are going to bloom
5. a. will end
   b. is going to end
6. a. will . . . buy
   b. are . . . going to buy
7. a. will . . . take
   b. am . . . going to take

PRACTICE 4, p. 38
1. Willingness
2. Prediction
3. Prediction
4. Prior plan
5. Willingness
6. Prior plan
7. Prediction

PRACTICE 5, p. 39
1. a. prior plan
2. b. decision of the moment
3. b. decision of the moment
4. a. prior plan
5. a. prior plan
6. b. decision of the moment

PRACTICE 6, p. 39
1. I'll call him
2. She's going to be / She'll be
3. I'm going to fly
4. We're going to the game
5. I'll open it
6. I'm going to teach / I will teach

PRACTICE 7, p. 39
1. will
2. are going to
3. will
4. A: Are you going to
   B: are going to
5. am going to
6. will
7. will
8. is going to
9. A: am going to
   B: will
10. B: am going to . . . will

PRACTICE 8, p. 40

Time Clauses
1. when you (return) from your trip
2. After the train (stops)
3. until it (gets) dark
4. As soon as the baby (is born)
5. When he (retires)
6. when you (are) eighteen years old
7. as soon as the late news (is) over
8. when the new semester (begins)

PRACTICE 9, p. 41

1. retire
2. rings
3. finish
4. take
5. arrives
6. graduates
7. is
8. hear
9. leave
10. get

PRACTICE 10, p. 41

1. b
2. a
3. b
4. a
5. a
6. a
7. a
8. b
9. a
10. a

PRACTICE 11, p. 42

1. will not / are not going to return . . . get
2. gets . . . will / is going to be
3. is not going to / won't be . . . learns . . . comes . . . asks
4. returns . . . is going to / will start
5. is going to / will build . . . is going to / will be . . . complete
6. hear . . . will let
7. will lend . . . finish
8. A: will / is going to be
   B: will / am going to be

PRACTICE 12, p. 43

1. 'm seeing
2. is having
3. is opening
4. is working
5. 're having
6. are attending

PRACTICE 13, p. 43

1. a, b, c
2. c
3. a, b
4. a, b, c
5. a, b
6. a

PRACTICE 14, p. 44

1. I'm sending
2. NC
3. I'm having
4. A: are you doing
   B: I'm studying
5. NC
6. are they getting
7. NC
8. we're moving
9. Is he teaching
10. A: I'm not sending
    B: I'm coming

PRACTICE 15, p. 45

1. will be sitting
2. will be flying
3. will be sleeping
4. will be snowing
5. will be watching

PRACTICE 16, p. 45

1. heals . . . will be playing
2. clear . . . will be standing
3. start . . . will be attending
4. have . . . will be shopping
5. will be attending . . . return

PRACTICE 17, p. 46

1. will already have risen
2. will have been riding
3. will already have landed
4. will have been listening
5. will have drunk
6. will have been flying
7. will have saved
8. will have taught

PRACTICE 18, p. 46

Note: *be going to* is also possible in place of *will*.
1. gets . . . will be shining
2. will brush . . . shower . . . will make
3. eats . . . will get
4. gets . . . will have drunk
5. will answer . . . will plan
6. will have called
7. will be attending
8. will go . . . will have
9. finishes . . . will take . . . returns
10. will work . . . . goes
11. leaves . . . will have attended
12. gets . . . will be playing . . . will be watching
13. will have been playing
14. will have . . . will talk
15. will watch . . . will put
16. goes . . . will have had . . . will be

CHAPTER 5: REVIEW OF VERB TENSES

PRACTICE 1, p. 48

1. has never flown
2. have been waiting . . . hasn't arrived
3. are . . . reach
4. didn't own . . . had owned
5. are having . . . has been
6. will have left . . . get
7. went . . . got . . . were dancing . . . were talking . . . was standing . . . had never met . . . introduced
8. was sitting . . . heard . . . got . . . looked . . . had just backed

PRACTICE 2, p. 48

1. am taking . . . leave . . . 'm going . . . leave . . . am going to go . . . is studying . . . has lived . . . knows . . . has promised . . . have never been . . . am looking
2. had been raining . . . dropped . . . is going to be . . . changes . . . wake . . . will be snowing

PRACTICE 3, p. 49

1. had been
2. met
3. had missed
4. was
5. got
6. took
7. was
8. had grown
9. was
10. was wearing
11. had changed
12. was still
13. asked
14. had gained
15. had turned
16. looked
17. were

PRACTICE 4, p. 49

Note: *be going to* is also possible in place of *will*.

1. will have been
2. will meet
3. will have missed
4. will be
5. get
6. will take
7. will no longer be
8. will have grown
9. will be
10. will probably wear
11. will have changed
12. will still be
13. will ask
14. will probably have gained
15. will have turned
16. will look
17. will be

PRACTICE 5, p. 50

Part I.

1. haven't seen
2. recuperating
3. happened
4. broke
5. was playing
6. is
7. doing
8. has
9. will / is going to be

Part II.

1. sent
2. haven't received
3. is not functioning
4. are trying
5. will / is going to start

PRACTICE 6, p. 51

1. used
2. use
3. does it consist
4. do teachers use
5. doesn't give
6. doesn't make
7. knows
8. sounds
9. talked
10. fell
11. agree
12. think
13. 'm taking
14. always asks
15. has been using
16. didn't realize / hadn't realized

PRACTICE 7, p. 52

1. a. is waiting
   b. has been waiting
   c. will have been waiting
2. a. is standing
   b. has been standing
   c. will have stood / will have been standing
   d. will have been standing

PRACTICE 8, p. 52

1. d. am waiting
2. c. has appeared
3. a. is in her room studying
4. b. do you think
5. c. has been working
6. c. 'm going to make
7. a. find
8. c. is
9. b. was watching
10. d. have existed
11. a. has been ringing
12. d. depends
13. a. 'm staying
14. b. has made
15. c. stepped
16. d. had been waiting
17. b. isn't going to exist
18. d. had never won
19. c. will have been studying

PRACTICE 9, p. 54

1. a. is seeing
2. a. I've talked
3. b. will be sleeping
4. c. have been boiling
5. c. had been making
6. a. don't believe
7. b. 'll help
8. b. has been
9. d. speaks
10. c. are becoming
11. a. hadn't been getting
12. a. reaches
13. a. lasted
14. c. have been working
15. c. will find
16. d. were sleeping
17. b. had lost
18. a. turn

CHAPTER 6: SUBJECT-VERB AGREEMENT

PRACTICE 1, p. 57

1. wears
2. are
3. beats
4. need
5. knows
6. magazines . . . years
7. are
8. subjects
9. There **are** . . . kinds
10. is
11. has
12. takes
13. like . . . get . . . workers . . . **don't** fit

PRACTICE 2, p. 58

1.	floats	Verb	Singular
2.	Boats	Noun	Plural
3.	lives	Verb	Singular
4.	friends	Noun	Plural
5.	eats	Verb	Singular
6.	Donuts	Noun	Plural
7.	Babies	Noun	Plural
8.	cries	Verb	Singular

PRACTICE 3, p. 58

1.	balls	/z/
2.	wishes	/əz/
3.	aunts	/s/
4.	flowers	/z/

5. parks /s/
6. touches /əz/
7. months /s/
8. trees /z/
9. dresses /əz/
10. valleys /z/
11. industries /z/
12. swallows /z/
13. cliffs /s/
14. baths /s/
15. bathes /z/

PRACTICE 4, p. 58
1. is
2. are   6. is
3. has   7. are
4. barks   8. is
5. bark   9. are
               10. is

PRACTICE 5, p. 59
1. is
2. are   6. are
3. is   7. are
4. are   8. is
5. is . . . is 9. is
               10. are

PRACTICE 6, p. 59
1. has
2. were   6. is
3. was   7. has
4. was   8. has
5. is   9. has (informal : have)

PRACTICE 7, p. 59
1. is
2. are   6. was
3. are   7. aren't
4. is   8. isn't
5. weren't   9. has
               10. have

PRACTICE 8, p. 60
1. are
2. is   8. are
3. is   9. are
4. is   10. is
5. is . . . is . . . is 11. are
6. isn't   12. are
7. isn't   13. are
                   14. are

PRACTICE 9, p. 60
1. is
2. like . . . drive
3. is
4. are . . . are
5. are . . . contains . . . are
6. costs
7. is . . . is . . . are
8. is . . . reminds . . . makes

PRACTICE 10, p. 61
1. has   9. is
2. takes   10. is
3. are . . . have 11. is
4. was . . . were 12. is . . . have
5. take   13. is
6. is   14. speak
7. are . . . is   15. use
8. has . . . are . . . were

PRACTICE 11, p. 62
1. vote
2. have participated
3. was
4. knows
5. speak . . . understand
6. are
7. do . . . broadcast
8. are
9. have been
10. has received . . . have gone
11. confirms
12. is . . . is
13. are
14. has
15. Aren't
16. is
17. begin   *4 states begin with the letter A:
    Alabama, Arkansas, Alaska, Arizona.
18. consists
19. have
20. is
21. Was

CHAPTER 7: NOUNS

PRACTICE 1, p. 63
1. cars   9. classes
2. women   10. feet
3. matches   11. heroes
4. mice   12. pianos
5. cities   13. videos
6. donkeys   14. bases
7. halves   15. bacteria
8. chiefs   16. series

PRACTICE 2, p. 63
1. potatoes   5. teeth
2. monkeys   6. beliefs
3. thieves . . . radios   7. fish
4. children   8. species . . . kilos

PRACTICE 3, p. 64
1. cares . . . feathers
2. occupations . . . Doctors . . . Pilots . . . airplanes . . .
   Farmers . . . crops . . . Shepherds . . .
3. designs buildings . . . digs . . . objects . . .
4. computers . . . Computers
5. factories . . . employs
6. Kangaroos . . . animals . . . continents . . . zoos
7. Mosquitos / Mosquitoes
8. tomatoes

PRACTICE 4, p. 64

1. a. parents'
   b. two
   c. parents + house
2. a. parent's
   b. one
   c. parent + concern
3. a. cats'
   b. many
   c. cats + eyes
4. a. cat's
   b. one
   c. cat + eyes
5. a. Mary's
   b. brother
   c. Mary + brother
6. a. Mary's
   b. brothers
   c. Mary + brothers
7. a. brothers'
   b. more than one
   c. brothers + team
8. a. brother's
   b. one
   c. brother + team

PRACTICE 5, p. 65

1. one
2. more than one
3. more than one
4. one
5. more than one
6. more than one
7. one
8. one

PRACTICE 6, p. 65

1. secretary**'s**
2. secretar**ies'**
3. cats**'**
4. cat**'s**
5. supervisors**'**
6. supervisor**'s**
7. bab**ies'**
8. baby**'s**
9. child**'s**
10. children**'s**
11. people**'s**
12. actors**'**
13. actor**'s**

PRACTICE 7, p. 66

1. mother's
2. grandmothers'
3. teacher's
4. boss'
5. employee's . . . employees'
6. men's . . . women's . . . children's . . . girls' . . . boys'

PRACTICE 8, p. 66

Adjectives

1. _____ expensive
2. ✓ theater
3. _____ small
4. ✓ movie
5. ✓ family
6. ✓ family
7. ✓ computer
8. ✓ hair
9. ✓ window
10. ✓ gas

PRACTICE 9, p. 66

1. groceries . . . grocery
2. chickens . . . chicken
3. tomato . . . tomatoes
4. pictures . . . picture
5. flower . . . flowers
6. drugs . . . drug
7. eggs . . . egg
8. two lanes . . . two-lane
9. five-minute . . . five minutes
10. sixty-year-old . . . sixty years old
11. truck . . . truck
12. computers . . . computer

PRACTICE 10, p. 67

1. a. kitchen table
2. c. bedroom tables
3. b. home office
4. a. home offices
5. b. office phone
6. c. bathroom sinks
7. a. vegetable garden
8. b. cherry trees

PRACTICE 11, p. 67

1. student handbook
2. birthday party
3. government check
4. airplane seats
5. cotton pajamas
6. hotel rooms
7. ten-month-old baby
8. three-day-trip
9. three-room-apartment
10. five-page paper
11. opera singer
12. stamp collector

PRACTICE 12, p. 68

Count	Noncount
1. eggs . . . bananas	food . . . bread . . . milk . . . coffee
2. letters . . . magazines . . . catalogs . . . bills	mail
3. Euros . . . pounds . . . dollars	money
4. ring . . . earrings	jewelry
5. language	vocabulary . . . grammar
6. table . . . chairs . . . umbrella	furniture

PRACTICE 13, p. 68

1. words
2. some
3. cars
4. much
5. sandwich
6. one
7. some
8. very

PRACTICE 14, p. 69

1. hair . . . eye**s**
2. No change.
3. No change.
4. No change.
5. No change.
6. class**es**
7. fax**es**

PRACTICE 15, p. 69

1. courage
2. some
3. shoes
4. garbage
5. glasses . . . glass
6. glasses . . . glass
7. some lost luggage . . . many
8. much . . . some
9. hills . . . lovely . . . damp
10. good

PRACTICE 16, p. 70

1. A
2. An
3. Ø Energy
4. A
5. An
6. Ø Fruit
7. Ø Sodium
8. Ø Air
9. Ø Rice
10. An
11. A
12. Ø Football
13. A
14. A

PRACTICE 17, p. 70

1.	a	8.	a
2.	some	9.	a
3.	an	10.	an
4.	some	11.	some
5.	a	12.	some
6.	some	13.	a
7.	some	14.	some

PRACTICE 18, p. 70

1.	b	4.	b
2.	a	5.	b
3.	a	6.	a

PRACTICE 19, p. 71

1. **The s**un . . . **the** sky
2. **The b**oy is about five years old, and **the** girl . . .
3. **Penguins** live in Antarctica. **Polar** bears . . .
4. Which is more important—**love** or **money**?
5. B: Do you have **a** dictionary? Look up **the** word in **the** dictionary.
6. B: . . . I didn't see **the** bee, but . . .

PRACTICE 20, p. 71

1. A: a . . . a
   B: a . . .
   A: The
2. A: the
3. A: a
4. A: a
   B: the
5. A: a
6. A: the
   B: a
   A: the
   B: the

PRACTICE 21, p. 72

1. Ø Lightning . . . a . . . Ø
2. a . . . the
3. Ø Circles . . . Ø
4. A . . . a . . . the . . . the
5. The . . . the . . . an
6. the . . . a . . . the . . . a . . . The . . . Ø
7. a . . . The . . . Ø

PRACTICE 22, p. 73

1. a. three . . . b. several . . . f. too many . . . g. a few . . .
   i. a number of
2. e. too much . . . h. a little . . . j. a great deal of . . . l. no

PRACTICE 23, p. 73

1.	many computer**s**	8.	many
2.	much	9.	is . . . much
3.	many child**ren** are	10.	much
4.	many **teeth**	11.	was . . . much
5.	many countr**ies**	12.	much
6.	much	13.	many . . . volcano**es** are
7.	much . . . much	14.	many speech**es**

PRACTICE 24, p. 74

1. a. pictures b. photographs d. ceramic bowls
2. a. milk c. magazines
3. b. people c. babies
4. a. food b. cream c. coffee
5. a. food b. pizza c. drinks
6. c. bottles of soda
7. a. thoughts c. ideas

8. c. fun d. work
9. a. people b. things c. professors
10. a. intelligence b. information d. education

PRACTICE 25, p. 75

1. a. We have a little money.
2. b. They know a few people.
3. b. She has a little patience.
4. a. I speak some Spanish.
5. b. Marta asked a few questions.

PRACTICE 26, p. 75

1.	b	5.	a
2.	a	6.	c
3.	b	7.	b
4.	a		

PRACTICE 27, p. 75

1.	some	a little
2.	some	a few
3.	some	a few
4.	some	a little
5.	not many	few
6.	some	a few
7.	almost no	little
8.	some	a few
9.	some . . . some	a little . . . a little
10.	some	a little
	some	a little

PRACTICE 28, p. 76

1.	state	6.	child . . . chimpanzees
2.	states	7.	neighbors
3.	puppies	8.	man
4.	puppy	9.	goose
5.	children	10.	women

PRACTICE 29, p. 77

1. person
2. **the** rights
3. **the** states
4. Each senator
5. Correct.
6. the small state**s**
7. the citizen**s** . . . correct
8. citizen

PRACTICE 30, p. 77

1.	of	7.	Ø
2.	Ø	8.	Ø
3.	of	9.	Ø . . . of . . . of
4.	Ø	10.	Ø . . . of
5.	Ø	11.	of . . . Ø
6.	of		

PRACTICE 31, p. 78

Across
3. All
4. some
6. man
8. Every

Down
1. Two
2. One
3. An
5. mice
6. many
7. men

CHAPTER 8: PRONOUNS

PRACTICE 1, p. 79
1. He → Bob
2. They → Mr. and Mrs. Nobriega
3. her → teacher
4. She → baby
5. It → kind
6. them → hawks
7. him → Mr. Frank
8. They → dog and cat

PRACTICE 2, p. 79
1. I
2. me
3. them . . . They
4. them
5. my . . . yours
6. his . . . hers . . . their
7. She and I . . . Our . . . us
8. me . . . its . . . it
9. they . . . They . . . their
10. its . . . its . . . It's

PRACTICE 3, p. 80
1. b   5. a, b
2. a   6. a, b
3. a, b   7. a, b
4. a

PRACTICE 4, p. 80
1. it . . . them   5. his or her / their
2. their   6. their . . . her
3. his . . . her   7. his or her . . .
4. it . . . They   its / their

PRACTICE 5, p. 81
1. ourselves   5. myself
2. herself   6. yourselves
3. himself   7. yourself
4. themselves

PRACTICE 6, p. 81
1. is angry at himself   5. talks to herself
2. introduce myself   6. fix itself
3. help yourself   7. laugh at ourselves
4. pat yourself   8. feeling sorry for himself

PRACTICE 7, p. 82
1. c. themselves   5. c. one
2. b. oneself   6. b. you
3. a. your   7. a. They
4. a. you

PRACTICE 8, p. 82
1. a. Another   7. a. Another
2. a. other   8. b. other
3. a. Others   9. b. The others
4. a. other   10. c. the other
5. b. the other   11. b. the other *
6. c. The others
   *Oregon, California, Alaska, Hawaii

PRACTICE 9, p. 83
1. another   4. another
2. another   5. another
3. another   6. another

PRACTICE 10, p. 84
1. d. each other   4. e. in other words
2. f. other than   5. b. after another
3. a. every other   6. c. the other day

PRACTICE 11, p. 84
(1) **Potatoes** are grown in most **countries**. They are one of the most widely grown **vegetables** in the world. They are very versatile; they can be prepared in many different **ways**.

(2) French **fries** are popular almost everywhere. Besides frying **them**, you can boil or bake **potatoes**. **Another** way people . . . and **other** kinds of dishes. **It's** . . . . from **potatoes**. There are still **other** ways . . . **processors** to make **products** such as **potato** chips and freeze-dried **potatoes**.

(3) **Potatoes** . . . where **they** were cultivated . . . 5,000 **years** ago. . . . potatoes were the **world's** first . . . the Incas carried **their** harvested **potatoes** . . . after **the** sun came up . . . the water out of them by stepping on **them**. This process **was** repeated for four or five **days** . . . stored **them** in **pots**. **The** Indians . . . .

CHAPTER 9: MODALS, PART 1

PRACTICE 1, p. 85
1. ~~to hear~~   hear
2. Correct.
3. ~~can heard~~   can hear
4. Correct.
5. ~~Do you can help~~ Can you help
6. Correct.
7. ~~oughts to~~   ought to
8. Correct.
9. ~~He supposed~~   He is supposed
10. Correct.
11. Correct.
12. ~~should to tell~~ should tell

PRACTICE 2, p. 85
1. c
2. a
3. f
4. e
5. b
6. d

PRACTICE 3, p. 86

1. a. cooking
   b. if I cooked
2. a. taking
   b. if we took
3. a. if I opened
   b. opening
4. a. joining
   b. if we joined
5. a. writing
   b. if I wrote

PRACTICE 4, p. 86

1. closing
2. if I closed
3. taking
4. if I went
5. leaving
6. cooking
7. if I made
8. finishing
9. if I used
10. recommending

PRACTICE 5, p. 87

	Necessity	Lack of Necessity	Prohibition
1.	✔		
2.			✔
3.		✔	
4.	✔		
5.		✔	
6.	✔		
7.	✔		
8.	✔		
9.			✔
10.		✔	

PRACTICE 6, p. 88

1. had to be
2. had to memorize
3. had to cancel . . . had
4. did you have to call
5. had to get
6. had to fasten

PRACTICE 7, p. 88

1. a
2. b
3. a
4. c
5. a
6. a
7. c
8. a
9. c
10. b

PRACTICE 8, p. 89

1. doesn't have to
2. had to
3. don't have to
4. had to
5. had to
6. do . . . have to
7. had to . . . didn't have to
8. do not have to
9. has to
10. have to

PRACTICE 9, p. 89

1. b
2. a
3. a
4. b
5. b
6. a
7. a
8. b

PRACTICE 10, p. 89

1. b
2. a
3. b, c
4. a
5. All are correct.
6. a

PRACTICE 11, p. 90

1. e
2. g
3. c
4. h
5. b
6. f
7. d
8. a

PRACTICE 12, p. 91

1. should have taken
2. should have turned
3. shouldn't have watched
4. should have visited
5. should have bought
6. should have ordered
7. shouldn't have come . . . should have stayed
8. shouldn't have changed . . . should have kept

PRACTICE 13, p. 91

1. should travel
2. should have gone
3. should paint . . . should be
4. shouldn't have painted
5. shouldn't have eaten
6. shouldn't drink . . . should drink
7. shouldn't have killed
8. should make

PRACTICE 14, p. 92

1. is supposed to arrive
2. am supposed to go
3. is supposed to be
4. was supposed to arrive
5. were supposed to come over
6. is supposed to run

PRACTICE 15, p. 93

1. yes
2. yes
3. no
4. yes
5. yes
6. no
7. yes
8. yes
9. no
10. no

PRACTICE 16, p. 93

1. d
2. g
3. a
4. j
5. b
6. e
7. f
8. c
9. i
10. h

PRACTICE 17, p. 93

1. Psychologist: could . . . could
   Psychologist: should
   Patient: should
2. Carl: could . . . could
   Waiter: should
   Carl: should
3. Mary: could . . . could
   Bob: should . . . should

PRACTICE 18, p. 94

Answers may vary.
1. **can speak**
2. **can** you help
3. **don't** have to come

4. **don't have to** pay
5. **must tell** the truth
6. should **get**
7. should **have** ordered
8. are suppose**d** to be
9. are suppose**d** to be
10. Why **don't you** join
11. **should** not eat
12. **Shall** we dance?
13. let's **not** dance

CHAPTER 10: MODALS, PART 2

PRACTICE 1, p. 95

	100%	About 95%	About 50% or less
1.			✓
2.		✓	
3.	✓		
4.		✓	
5.			✓
6.	✓		
7.		✓	
8.			✓
9.			✓
10.			✓

PRACTICE 2, p. 95
1. a. must
2. b. could
3. b. may . . . may
4. a. must
5. b. may
6. a. must
7. b. may
8. b. may be
9. b. could be
10. a. am
11. b. must be
12. b. is

PRACTICE 3, p. 96
1. f. must not like
2. a. can't be him
3. c. may not be
4. d. may not speak
5. b. can't be true
6. e. must not get

PRACTICE 4, p. 97
1. b
2. a
3. b
4. a
5. a
6. b

PRACTICE 5, p. 98
1. must not have remembered
2. couldn't have been
3. may / might not have left
4. must not have heard
5. may / might not have had
6. couldn't have happened

PRACTICE 6, p. 98
1. must have driven
2. must have been / must be
3. must not have known
4. must be
5. must have left
6. must have gone
7. must need
8. must have hurt

PRACTICE 7, p. 99
1. a
2. a
3. b
4. a
5. b
6. a

PRACTICE 8, p. 100
1. e
2. j
3. a
4. f
5. b
6. d
7. i
8. c
9. h
10. g

PRACTICE 9, page 100
1. will
2. should
3. will
4. should
5. will
6. should
7. must
8. should

PRACTICE 10, p. 101
Answers may vary.
1. could be working
2. should be flying
3. might be sleeping
4. must be kidding
5. must have been kidding
6. might be hiking
7. may not be dating

PRACTICE 11, p. 102
1. c
2. c
3. b
4. b
5. c
6. c
7. b
8. c
9. b
10. b

PRACTICE 12, p. 103
Answers may vary.
1. a. It should arrive soon.
   b. It may / might / could have taken off late.
   c. We should have called the airport.
2. a. It may be for me.
   b. It's for me.
   c. It can't be for me.
3. a. He should have responded.
   b. He may not have gotten it.
   c. He must not have gotten it.
   d. He couldn't have gotten it.
4. a. The dishwasher may / might / could be leaking.
   b. It can't be the dishwasher.
   c. A pipe must be broken.
   d. You should call a plumber.
   e. You don't have to call a plumber.

PRACTICE 13, p. 103
1. can't
2. couldn't
3. can
4. couldn't
5. can't
6. could . . . can't

PRACTICE 14, p. 104
1. would fall . . . would throw
2. would always yell . . . would come
3. would always bring
4. would always wipe
5. would stay . . . would sleep
6. would tell . . . would listen

PRACTICE 15, p. 104
1. would rather not say
2. would rather have gone
3. would rather have studied
4. would rather not eat
5. would rather have
6. would rather be sailing

PRACTICE 16, p. 105
1. have to get
2. should be able to complete
3. won't have to stand
4. will you be able to leave
5. am not going to be able to graduate
6. must not have been able to get

CHAPTER 11: THE PASSIVE

PRACTICE 1, p. 106
1. are
2. is being
3. has been
4. was
5. was being
6. had been
7. will be
8. is going to be
9. will have been
10. has been
11. was
12. are being
13. will be
14. had been
15. will have been
16. are
17. is going to be
18. were being

PRACTICE 2, p. 107

		Subject	Verb
1.	A	Henry	visited
2.	P	The park	was visited
3.	A	Olga	was reading
4.	A	Philippe	has read
5.	P	Bambi	has been read
6.	A	Whales	swim
7.	P	Whales	were hunted
8.	P	The answer	won't be known
9.	A	I	know
10.	P	Two new houses	were built
11.	A	A famous architect	designed
12.	P	Television	was invented
13.	P	The World Cup	is seen
14.	A	Television	has expanded

PRACTICE 3, p. 107
1. is written
2. is being written
3. has been written
4. was written
5. was being written
6. had been written
7. will be written
8. is going to be written
9. will have been written
10. Was . . . written
11. Will . . . be written
12. Has . . . been written

PRACTICE 4, p. 107
Part I.
1. was painted by Picasso
2. are flown by experienced pilots
3. is going to be sung by a famous singer
4. has been accepted by Yale University
5. will be examined by the doctor
6. is being questioned by the defense attorney
7. was bitten by a dog
8. was being fed by the mother bird
9. won't be persuaded by his words
10. wasn't painted by me . . . painted by Laura
11. owned by Mrs. Crane
    isn't owned by her father anymore
12. weren't signed by me
    was signed by someone else

Part II.
13. is going to clean my teeth
14. Did . . . send that email
15. don't celebrate the Fourth of July
16. Has . . . sold your house yet
17. haven't caught the thief
18. are cleaning the carpets

PRACTICE 5, p. 109

	Verb	Object Of Verb	Passive Sentence
1.	will pay	the bill	The bill will be paid by Al.
2.	will arrive	Ø	Ø
3.	supplies	towels	Towels are supplied by the hotel.
4.	happen	Ø	Ø
5.	noticed	my error	My error was noticed by everyone.
6.	arrived	Ø	Ø
7.	didn't surprise	me	I was not surprised by the news.
8.	Did . . . surprise	you	Were you surprised by the news?
9.	Do . . . exist	Ø	Ø
10.	died	Ø	Ø
11.	told	the story	The story was told by an old man.
12.	hasn't rained	Ø	Ø

PRACTICE 6, p. 109

1. b. will be notified
2. b. didn't remember
3. c. was built
4. a. is visited
5. b. don't agree
6. c. will be invaded
7. c. been accepted
8. b. died
9. a. live
10. c. was felt
11. b. was ruled
12. a. walked

PRACTICE 7, p. 110

1. b
2. b
3. a
4. b
5. a

PRACTICE 8, p. 110

1. was invented . . . told
2. was established . . . was given . . . still attend
3. is known . . . is related . . . live . . . became . . . were killed . . . were saved
4. originated . . . like . . . gives . . . was valued . . . was used . . . were treated . . . is believed

PRACTICE 9, p. 111

1. The chefs prepared the food.
2. The food was prepared yesterday.
3. The rain stopped.
4. A rainbow appeared in the sky.
5. The documents were sent to you yesterday.
6. My lawyer sent the documents to me.
7. The winner of the election was announced on TV.
8. I didn't agree with you about this.
9. What happened yesterday?
10. Something wonderful happened to me.
11. The trees died of a disease.
12. The trees were killed by a disease.
13. A disease killed the trees.
14. I was accepted at the University of Chicago.
15. I was recommended for a scholarship.

PRACTICE 10, p. 112

1. can't be
2. should be washed
3. should have been washed
4. to be finished
5. must have been built
6. have to be paid . . . must be sent
7. be permitted
8. ought to be painted

PRACTICE 11, p. 112

1. should be made
2. should make
3. should have been made
4. couldn't talk
5. couldn't have talked
6. must be registered
7. must register
8. has to be paid . . . had better not send
9. must have been
10. may have been

PRACTICE 12, p. 113

1. g. locked
2. e. closed
3. a. finished
4. h. broken
5. b. lost
6. c. crowded
7. f. gone
8. d. turned on

PRACTICE 13, p. 113

1. is interested in
2. depends on
3. is married to
4. is scared of
5. bores
6. are made of
7. is composed of
8. is located in
9. are doing

PRACTICE 14, p. 113

1. in
2. for
3. about
4. in
5. to
6. of
7. with
8. with
9. with
10. with
11. of
12. to

PRACTICE 15, p. 114

1. ~~was arrived~~ arrived
2. ~~injured~~ were injured
3. ~~with~~ to
4. ~~with~~ about
5. ~~interesting~~ interested
6. surprise surprised
7. Correct.
8. ~~We lost.~~ We are lost.
9. ~~might helped~~ might be helped
10. ~~is been~~ is being
11. ~~was happened~~ happened
12. ~~Will be fixed the refrigerator~~ Will the refrigerator be fixed
13. ~~must been remembers~~ must have been remembered

PRACTICE 16, p. 114

1. crowded
2. hungry
3. lost
4. scared
5. dressed
6. hurt
7. invited
8. fat
9. stopped
10. elected

PRACTICE 17, p. 115

1. excited
2. exciting
3. shocking
4. shocked
5. exhausting . . . exhausted
6. boring . . . bored
7. confused . . . confusing
8. interesting
9. interested
10. thrilling . . . thrilled

PRACTICE 18, p. 115

1. a. fascinating
   b. fascinated
2. a. exhausting
   b. exhausted
3. a. disappointed
   b. disappointing

PRACTICE 19, p. 115

1. a, d
2. a, b
3. b, c
4. b, d
5. b, c

PRACTICE 20, p. 116

1. frustrating
2. grown . . . irritating
3. washing
4. writing
5. written
6. depressing . . . depressed
7. entertaining
8. known . . . spilt
9. comforting . . . Barking
10. inspiring . . . United . . . divided